ISBN: 9781290774369

Published by:
HardPress Publishing
8345 NW 66TH ST #2561
MIAMI FL 33166-2626

Email: info@hardpress.net
Web: http://www.hardpress.net

THE DRAMATIC WORKS OF
ST. JOHN HANKIN

THE DRAMATIC WORKS OF
ST. JOHN HANKIN

WITH AN INTRODUCTION BY JOHN DRINKWATER

VOLUME
ONE

LONDON
MARTIN SECKER
NUMBER FIVE JOHN STREET
ADELPHI
MCMXII

Dear Mrs. Hankin

Those of St. John Hankin's plays that were dedicated to any one were, of course, inscribed to you ; and in terms that made the playwright's general purpose in this direction sufficiently clear. Had he lived to see this collected record of the work that he did for the theatre, there is but one name that could have received the rightful homage of dedication, but with this comment my right in the matter ends. I may, however, be allowed to inscribe my work in preparing this edition to you who have sought so loyally to establish the reputation of the dramatist that it celebrates.

Very faithfully yours,

John Drinkwater

CONTENTS OF
VOLUME ONE

INTRODUCTION

I : A

INTRODUCTION

St. John Emile Clavering Hankin died in 1909, at the age of thirty-nine. To discuss the circumstances of his death would be an irrelevancy that could serve no useful purpose. The only word that need be said in this connection is in answer to an ill-considered suggestion that the event was hastened by some sense of disappointment, an unsatisfied hunger for recognition. All artists of real distinction are alike in being proud of their work; they differ only, for temperamental reasons, in the manner of expressing their pride. Reserve in this matter is not necessarily the virtue of modesty, nor, on the other hand, do we think the less of the makers who have foretold that their rhymes should be more durable than marble monuments. St. John Hankin was proud of his work, and made frank avowal of the fact. "You always think so well of your own plays, Hankin," said a colleague. "Of course I do," was the reply, "otherwise I shouldn't continue to write them." The statement implies no undue self-satisfaction. He was not easily content with the thing he had written, and was a finely conscientious workman in revision and the search for rightness in balance and form. But the task done, he was glad to stand by it, and said so. It is, however, a deep injustice to his memory to suppose that this frankness sprang from any overweening concern

3

for his immediate reputation, and mere folly to add that it affords any clue as to the cause of his last act. In the first place, artists do not die of wounded pride. Keats was not "snuffed out by an article," but by an organic disease, and even Chatterton's tragedy might have been averted by a few shillings a week. Secondly, Hankin had already received a large measure of the only kind of recognition that he valued. He was not forced to write for money, and he neither expected nor wished his plays to be readily accepted by the general public. He was deliberately in the camp of the pioneers, and did not look for the rewards of conformity. But his work had won the approval of progressive audiences, and had been acclaimed by the most liberal critical opinion. The new repertory movement in the theatre, upon which he himself exercised so important an influence, was in turn recognising him as one of its most notable products. His name was one of credit among the people who were seeking to quicken a stage that had grown moribund, and the knowledge that this was so gave him just and genuine pleasure. He was working with a clearly defined aim, and he was achieving his purpose as rapidly as any man can hope to do. St. John Hankin the neglected and disappointed dramatist is a myth. At the time of his death he was winning and enjoying the best kind of success, and his end was one of those untimely accidents of temperament and physical circumstance that we are wise to accept without too curious analysis. Nor would it be profitable to speculate as to what might have been added to his achievement had his life

4

been prolonged. We have to consider his work as it stands, and examine the grounds upon which its claims to permanence may be established.

The decadence of English drama, that began with the passing away of the Elizabethans and has been arrested only in our own day, has commonly been supposed to have been the penalty paid for the neglect of life. By decadence we do not mean a lack of superficial and momentary success. Every age has produced its harvest of plays that would attract and hold large, if uncritical, audiences, and they have not always been wholly bad plays. The great mass of them have, indeed, been radically deficient in true dramatic sense, and, by substituting violent events and action for ideas and character focussed into action, have vulgarised a great art. But a substantial minority have been the product of sincere observation and some feeling for character. And yet, the plays written in England between the end of the Shakespearian age and the beginning of the present generation that are of indisputable excellence when put to the test of the stage and also survive the processes of time might be numbered at a bare dozen ; certainly no more. The Restoration dramatists would contribute two or three between them ; Goldsmith claims one, perhaps two ; Sheridan two, possibly three. The list is not easily to be lengthened. On the other hand, most of the poets of high rank have written plays, and in many cases plays that are immortal but only by virtue of qualities that are not stage qualities. Action is not essential to the stage, but

5

in its absence there must at least be some direct progression of idea or spiritual conflict that shall perform its office of holding the attention of an audience. The poets have, justly, thrown action from its usurped station in drama, but they have failed either to use it in proper measure or to substitute its equivalent, and for this reason their influence has been deflected from the theatre. We have, then, the few plays that have held the stage and still live ; the poets' plays that are imperishable but do not fulfil the requirements of the stage ; the large number of plays that sought only a momentary and sensational success and could not, by reason of their essential abuse of dramatic art, achieve more. And there are left those plays, cumulatively through the generations a large number, that had in them some sincerity and conscience and also a measure of fitness for the stage, and have yet passed into oblivion. If we ask ourselves why these plays have perished, we find that the suggestion that the stage had divorced itself from life leaves the question unanswered. The truth is that the stage fell upon evil days not because it divorced itself from life, but because it divorced itself from literature. Literature means style in the expression of life, and if we look at those plays that paid some heed to life and adjusted it with skill to the theatre, we find that the one supreme quality that they lacked is style. The poets have always brought this quality to the drama, but they have neglected the rightful demands of the stage in other things. Drama that shall succeed in the theatre and also be a permanent addition to the art of the world can only spring

6

from the union of an understanding of stage-craft and the faculty of at once seeing and apprehending life and character, or at least manners, and bringing to their expression that discipline of language which is style.

The loftiest style is employed in the service of poetry. When the impulse to express the thing seen passes beyond a certain degree of urgency the expression takes on a new quality of rhythmical force, shaping itself generally into verse. The difference between fine prose and fine verse is fundamentally rather one of urgency, of intensity, than of beauty. The greatest verse may have a loveliness that is not to be found in the greatest prose, but this beauty is a result of the essential distinction, not the distinction itself. It is for this reason that our new drama, full as it is of hope and even achievement, does not yet make any serious challenge to that of the Elizabethans. With two or three exceptions, the plays that we have produced have not been forced by the sheer strength of their begetting impulse into poetic form. But many of them have already been so forced into style, a style lower than the highest, but of clear authenticity, and these are plays too that are fitted to the requirements of stage presentation. We have not yet regained our lost estate, but we are realising that it is worth regaining, and already the result is a quickening of our dramatic perception. A knowledge of life and the theatre is no longer considered sufficient equipment for the playwright, and men of real literary gifts, men, that is, with the gift of style, are seeking first to understand the theatre so that they may bring their labours to its service. The stage is renewing its old relation to literature, and that is the most wholesome thing that has happened to the stage for three centuries. It was St. John Hankin's privilege and distinction to be one of the first dramatists in England to help in the establishment of this reunion. The great worth of his plays lies not in their philosophy; after all, the Eustace Jacksons of the world have never lacked persuasive and perfectly logical advocates, and Mrs. Cassilis only invents a new trick to emphasise a very old truth. It is not in the technical excellence of their stage-craft; they are often merciless to producer and actors, and St. John Hankin's stage has a habit of resolving itself into a veritable chess-board. They will take a permanent place in the theatre because they are, on the whole and in spite of their flaws in this respect, constructed for action on the stage, and their expression of the dramatist's view of life is vibrant with style from beginning to end.

The distinction between writing that has this quality of style and writing that lacks it is not the distinction between the same thing well and ill said; it is the distinction between two entirely different things. It is the difference between the dull acceptance which is knowledge and the swift realisation which is imaginative thought. The former might induce a man to speak of one dead as, say, having " escaped from a very worrying world and the annoyances of jealous and unjust people and the disappointments of life in general," but it is clearly a mistake to suppose that he experiences

8

or expresses the same spiritual emotion as the man who cries out :

> He has outsoared the shadow of our night ;
> Envy and calumny and hate and pain,
> And that unrest which men miscall delight
> Can touch him not and torture not again ;
> From the contagion of the world's slow stain
> He is secure, and now can never mourn
> A heart grown cold, a head grown grey in vain ;
> Nor when the spirit's self has ceased to burn
> With sparkless ashes load an unlamented urn.

The difference here is that between formal assent and vision. Ultimately it is sincerity that creates style, and sincerity has been lost to our theatre save for brief interludes until these new dramatists once again began to write not from rumour but from conscience. Those momentarily successful plays that presented life not altogether distorted and at the same time fulfilled the technical requirements of the stage perished because their virtues were not really sincere. Their makers said the right thing because it was commonly reported to be the right thing and not from conviction, and consequently said it ill, which, artistically, amounted to not saying it at all. Lacking the sincerity which should result in style, they lacked the power of complete utterance, and in art a thing either is completely said or it does not exist. We must not, of course, confuse completeness with over-elaboration ; reticence is often the spirit of style. Completeness implies the embodiment of the creative ecstasy of the artist with the actual statement made, and this ecstasy cannot exist, of course, apart from the strictest sincerity.

Among the many vague generalities that have gained currency among us none is more thoughtless than the pronouncement that art should imitate nature. It should do nothing of the sort. When Oscar Wilde asserted that, on the contrary, nature imitates art, he was only refuting what he knew to be a shallow conventionalism with his usual fantastic gaiety. It would need a good deal of ingenious sophistry for such an ideal to find a more excellent realisation than the photograph and the gramophone. Nature—life—becomes art only by concentration and selection. A play focusses into two hours the selected and concentrated experience of many lives, and it finds an expression that is correspondingly artificial and purged. Its failure to do this is the measure of its failure as a work of art. It is for this reason that the greatest drama is the poetic drama, where the expression reaches the highest artificiality, and the symbol most consistently takes the place of the traditional formula of speech. To say that a play is true to life, in the sense that it is an unshaped extract from life, and that its people speak in life-like speech, is utterly to condemn it. Those plays of which I have spoken frequently preserved, when they were not couched in fustian rhetoric, the most exact parallel to the daily use of conversation. The point is that in either case they were the result of hearsay and not of imagination ; they accepted without question either the false rumours of literature which their authors had never examined or the current speech of daily life which had lost all freshness and a great deal of its meaning. Ibsen paused to consider this question before making his plays, or perhaps it would be nearer the truth to say that, bringing real creative impulse to his work, he necessarily rejected at the outset the false doctrines of common acceptance. St. John Hankin was one of the men who, consciously or not, profited by the example. His characters are as far removed as possible in expression from a debased tradition of literary grandiosity, and, on the other hand, they are far from reaching high imaginative utterance. But their speech is, nevertheless, definitely one of the imagination :

HENRY. It was extremely undignified and quite unnecessary. If you had simply come up to the front door and rung the bell you would have been received just as readily.

EUSTACE. I doubt it. In fact, I doubt if I should have been received at all. I might possibly have been given a bed for the night, but only on the distinct understanding that I left early the next morning. Whereas now nobody talks of my going. A poor invalid ! In the doctor's hand ! Perfect quiet essential. No. My plan was best.

HENRY. Why didn't that fool Glaisher see through you ?

EUSTACE. Doctors never see through their patients. It's not what they're paid for, and it's contrary to professional etiquette. [HENRY *snorts wrathfully*.] Besides, Glaisher's an ass, I'm glad to say.

HENRY [*fuming*]. It would serve you right if I told the Governor the whole story.

EUSTACE. I daresay. But you won't. It wouldn't be cricket. Besides, I only told you on condition you kept it to yourself.

HENRY [*indignant*]. And so I'm to be made a partner in your fraud. The thing's a swindle, and I've got to take a share in it.

EUSTACE. Swindle ? Not a bit. You've lent a hand—without intending it—to reuniting a happy family circle. Smoothed the way for the Prodigal's return. A very beautiful trait in your character.

HENRY [*grumpy*]. What I don't understand is why you told me all this. Why in heaven's name didn't you keep the whole discreditable story to yourself ?

EUSTACE [*with flattering candour*]. The fact is I was pretty sure you'd find me out. The Governor's a perfect owl, but you've got brains—of a kind. You can see a thing when it's straight before your nose. So I thought I'd let you into the secret from the start, just to keep your mouth shut.

HENRY. Tck! [*Thinks for a moment.*] And what are you going to do now you are at home ?

EUSTACE [*airily*]. Do, my dear chap ? Why, nothing.

[*And on the spectacle of* EUSTACE'S *smiling self-assurance, and* HENRY'S *outraged moral sense, the curtain falls.*]

That is not the speech of daily life. No two brothers ever talked to each other or could talk so. There is in their conversation something added to the actual argument between the two men, and this addition is the imagination of St. John Hankin. Eustace and Henry Jackson are not wholly creatures of their own independent being ; they exist partly in terms of their creator's temperament and vision, and they justly and inevitably bear witness to this fact in their utterance. The philosophy that finds a spark of the Godhead in every man is relatively applicable to art. The creature bears in him some token of the creator, and unless he does so he is deprived of his proudest right. The dramatist whose characters are set out photographically, not reflected through the distinctive medium of his own personality, does not create at all and he has no claim to consideration as an artist. He may then catch the verisimilitude of speech, but the spirit with which he should invest words must necessarily be beyond his consciousness, and his expression will remain untranslated into style.

It is a curious fact that this essential condition of all art should have been so often overlooked in dramatic criticism whilst its importance has been consistently recognised in the discussion of the other arts. A poem or a picture or a statue is accounted as deficient in the finer parts of its being unless it bears in its composition some signature of its source, and yet for some obscure reason we have been asked to consider it as a virtue that a play should be as a bough lopped from the tree of life, unshaped and showing no pressure of the artist's hand. The great dramatists have never bestowed their approval on this monstrous notion by their practice. The art of the dramatist is, indeed, more essentially objective than that of his fellows, but objectivity in art does not imply an abortive dissociation of the thing seen from the eyes that see. Strangely enough, St. John Hankin, who realised this truth always in his art, appeared to lend support to its violation in an essay otherwise full of admirable reason. " It is the dramatist's business," he says, " to represent life, not to argue about it." It is, perhaps, not special pleading to suggest that in speaking of argument he had in mind the distortion of life to make it conform to fore-ordained ends. The sentence is to be found in the " Note on Happy Endings," where he justly resents the sentimental intrusion of expediency on the dramatist's conception of truth. His protest would seem to be made rather against the sophistical devices of argument than against argument in the shape of commentary, but, with so important an issue at stake, he would have done well to have considered his statement more carefully. However this may be, it is clear that all dramatists who have written sincerely have not only represented life, but argued about it. The very texture of their expression, as in the passage that has been quoted, is an implicit argument about life, in that it knits up the artist's temperament into the speech of his characters. But the argument has always been explicit also, a deliberate as well as an incidental commentary. The Greek chorus was, fundamentally, a device employed by the poet whereby he might exercise this privilege of argument. The characters that he created might be allowed to work out their own destiny as far as he could enable them to do so by virtue of his experience of life ; but he was careful to reserve his right of commentary upon the process. The æsthetic value of this determination is obvious. Our demand of the artist is that he should show us not life, but his vision of life. The earliest English drama made frank allowance of this right, an allowance too frank, indeed, to be artistically sound. The explicit argument was not clearly cut off from the characterisation as it had been by the Greeks, nor was it yet woven into the fibre of the characterisation in the manner attempted by the Elizabethans. And the Elizabethans themselves were not blameless in this matter. In rejecting the classical model Shakespeare set himself the most difficult of his technical problems. His magnificent genius justified its own choice, but the soliloquy was, inherently, a less perfect artistic form than the chorus. The greatest difficulty in the loyal presentation of Shakespeare's plays is in dealing convincingly with these choric soliloquies. To adopt the line of least resistance and cut them

14

out, as is commonly done, is merely to maim the poet. Shakespeare felt the artistic necessity of comment upon his creations, but in blurring the dividing line between his dramatic and choric statement instead of defining it sharply he deprived his audience of help to which it has a legitimate claim. But difficulty is no excuse for inefficiency, and no Shakespearian production is of the slightest æsthetic value that does not honestly seek to meet the difficulty instead of resorting to cowardly evasion.

The demands of art upon the artist are inexorable. The artist finds certain requirements imposed upon him by his work from which there is no escape. And one of these is this necessity of the chorus, or the poet's argument in drama. The whole significance of the chorus in the drama of the theatre had fallen into neglect and oblivion, because the plays of the theatre were being written by men who had no sincerity of artistic impulse. And then, as soon as men once more bring their conscience to this work and write sincerely as artists, we find the necessity reasserting itself in spite of any reasoned denial. The new dramatists, of whom St. John Hankin was one of the ablest and sincerest, seemed to be determined that the construction of their plays should follow a false tradition at least in this, that it should not allow anything to interfere with the development of the action. But they were too good artists to be able to carry out their own determination. Being sincere, and creating characters instead of cutting them out with a pair of scissors, they found it necessary, as we have seen, to invest them with something of their own temper, and that in itself wholesomely disturbed the mechanical continuity that had become a fetish. Here was the beginning of regeneration, and the beginning forced its own growth. Having brought implicit argument back to the drama, they felt an artistic desire for argument that was explicit. Not being quite sure of themselves, they refrained from satisfying the desire openly, and they started a new tradition, which will, it is safe to prophesy, prove nothing more than the prelude to a return to the frank acceptance of an essential artistic necessity. They invented the stage direction. Not the old direction that set out a stage and brought people on to it and off again, but a new full-bodied thing that enabled them to do something which their art compelled them to do.

GENERAL BONSOR [*too broken with the world's ingratitude to protest further*]. Boring ! [*Follows* MISS TRIGGS, *shaking his poor old head. There is a pause while we realise that one of the most tragic things in life is to be a bore—and to know it.* MRS. EVERSLEIGH, *however, not being cursed with the gift of an imaginative sympathy, wastes no pity on the General. Instead of this she turns to her sister, and, metaphorically speaking, knocks her out of the ring.*]

That is pure chorus, and nothing else. And again :

MRS. JACKSON. But what became of your money, dear ? The thousand pounds your father gave you ?
EUSTACE. I lost it.
MRS. JACKSON [*looking vaguely round as if* EUSTACE *might have dropped it somewhere on the carpet, in which case, of course, it ought to be picked up before some one treads on it*]. Lost it ?

This is as clear in intention as a chorus of Trojan women, and instances are to be found on nearly
16

every page of the authentic artists who are re-establishing the credit of our theatre. They are, indeed, to be found on the pages only, not yet on the stage in their complete and rightful authority; but the fact that they are conceived and written is evidence of the return of a perfectly sound instinct. The most complete attempts to give this elemental desire natural expression that have yet been made in modern drama are, perhaps, to be found in certain of Mr. Yeats's plays and in the Gaffer of Mr. Masefield's *Nan*.

The Two Mr. Wetherbys was written in 1902. Before that date St. John Hankin had worked as dramatic and literary critic, and was known as a contributor to *Punch*. He had by him, too, the usual sheaf of plays, and was wise enough to leave them in their pigeon-holes when his reputation as a dramatist might have lent them a value not their own. He looked upon *The Two Mr. Wetherbys* as the first achievement by which he cared to stand. *Mr. Punch's Dramatic Sequels* was published in 1901, but its wit is relatively immature and not comparable with that of his *Lost Masterpieces*, published three years later. Between 1902 and his death he wrote seven plays and began an eighth, and it is upon these that his reputation rests. In *The Two Mr. Wetherbys* certain of his qualities appear almost in their full development, others scarcely at all. The faculty of writing dialogue, the style, the salty wit and the debonair, faintly cynical philosophy of life, are all there. But there is as yet nothing of the deeper humour and the real tenderness that were to throw their gracious charity over the mocking satire of the later plays, nor is the artistic sincerity yet perfect. It is the only one of his plays that has a conventionally happy ending of the kind that he laughed at so vigorously in the preface from which I have already quoted, and it is the only one that ends unsatisfactorily. In sending Dick and Constantia off to inevitable domestic tribulation he may have had his tongue in his cheek, but, if so, the humour was too subtle to be safe, involving as it did a direct negation of his own conviction. The whole question of the destiny of the artists' creations is necessarily one that each artist must decide for himself. St. John Hankin quite rightly decided that the romantic conclusions popularly favoured were false. It does not follow that they are false to life or to another artist's view of life, but simply that they were false for him. They are, indeed, commonly enough so contrived as to fail altogether in artistic conviction, but this does not affect their radical fitness when conceived by the right temperament. Eustace Jackson's engagement to Stella Faringford would, doubtless, have trebled the popularity of *The Return of the Prodigal*, but any balance in our knowledge of life, or, more particularly, in our knowledge of Hankin's vision of life, precludes us from deploring his refusal to sanction such an event ; but we are, none the less, profoundly disturbed by the accident that prevents the consummation of Romeo's love for Juliet. It is the prerogative of passion to take no account of institutions or social expediency. Great poets in their most passionate seasons create without reference to

18

anything save their own burning conception. Love's moment is for them an immortal term which is independent of any subsequent reaction or retribution. But it was Hankin's limitation as an artist that he could not see life detached from such institutions and expediencies. He could see clearly but not very deeply ; his characters are alive and considered from many points of view, but he was never able to divest them of the rags of circumstance. The danger of passion was, in consequence, a more real thing for him than its glory. Much as he did for the renascence of drama in many ways, he was yet far from bringing reason under the fine subjection of the imagination. Eustace's marriage to Stella would have been a catastrophe only because these people were created by Hankin's temperament ; a greater imagination might have made such an event triumphant. An artist, however, is not to be censured for his limitations, but only for his refusal to recognise and work within them. Of the higher things of passion Hankin was incapable, but he was wisely content to acknowledge the incapacity, and, working consistently within his powers, he rediscovered certain artistic principles of first-rate importance, in the expression of an impulse not of the highest order, yet in itself of no mean value.

The Return of the Prodigal, which followed the *Wetherbys,* was written in 1904. Not only have the qualities that were found in the earlier play matured, but there are new qualities discovered. If it was not given to him to be passionate, Hankin here shows that he could encompass a quite rare tenderness. Mrs. Jackson, first-cousin to the Lady Denison of a later date, is conceived with a charity that has in it no trace of cynicism. She is not a central figure in the play, and yet she is, it seems to me, more completely imagined than any other character in the whole of Hankin's work. This is not to say that she is the most striking of his people, but there is in her just that subtlety of presentment that is the product not of deliberation but of uncurbed artistic instinct. She is there for no other purpose than to satisfy the dramatist's impulse to embody a type for which he clearly had no common affection. Eustace and Henry, Samuel Jackson and even his daughter Violet, admirably fashioned as they are, are yet moved by a purpose that is not wholly their own, and answer in some measure to the dictates of the dramatist's formal reason. But Mrs. Jackson is a complete creation, arguing nothing, doing nothing, merely being, and in her Hankin approaches poetic imagination in conception if not in utterance. And it is noteworthy that, moving on this higher artistic plane, her influence upon the other characters of the play is more authentically dramatic than is that commonly operating between Hankin's people. The conflict between Eustace and his father and brother is, again, primarily one of the reasons, just as, in a lesser degree, is that between him and his sister. They have a definite and circumstantial problem to solve, and they argue the matter out consistently in terms of their own personalities. But Eustace's relation to his mother is an emotional one, and consequently far more moving. " Dear old mater. She's not clever, but for real goodness of heart I don't know her equal." Speaking of her he becomes, for a moment, greater than himself, concerned with simple and fundamental and not complex and superficial things.

In 1905 two plays were written, *The Charity that Began at Home* and *The Cassilis Engagement*. If Hankin saw life in something less than heroic proportions, he was at least able to apply an almost faultless logic to the life that he did see. His world was circumscribed, but he purged it thoroughly of shams ; and if to do this is not the highest function of the artist, it is one of the most worthy functions of the artist who professes no kinship with the greatest. And it is certainly to be accounted to him artistically as a virtue that, although he exposed what he considered to be ethical and social fallacies in some measure by statement and argument, he did so in a larger measure by the operation of character. In other words, although he intuitively realised the necessity of the chorus in drama, he was also able to preserve a just balance between chorus and action. The questions that confront Lady Denison and Mrs. Cassilis are considered by the dramatist not only with fine subtlety and mental precision, but also with a quite notable instinct for dramatic form. Generally speaking, the impulse behind the plays is not sufficiently imaginative to raise them save at rare intervals to the level of a Mrs. Jackson, but the instinct that directed the adjustment of the relations of the dramatist's reflections to the action of his characters was in nearly every case sound. Whilst the dramatist may and should argue about life, it is not his business to argue about ideas in the abstract. If he uses his characters merely as mouth-pieces for the exploitation of abstractions he abuses them ; his privilege of choric commentary is justly exercised only when it is confined to the contemplation of ideas that shape themselves out of the action of his characters ; when, in other words, it is applied to the general only as it is resolved from the particular. It is not for Œdipus, crushed, blind and bereft, driven from his fellows, to be conscious of more than his immediate misery ; life, for him, has become the present moment of fierce pain and nothing more. But the poet, seeing his creation set against the whole of experience, remembering this man's beginning and story and all men's hope, can draw from the disastrous moment an abstract idea purged into peace, almost into exultation :

Ye citizens of Thebes, behold ; 'tis Œdipus that passeth here,
Who read the riddle-word of Death, and mightiest stood of mortal
    men,
And Fortune loved him and the folk that saw him turned and looked
    again.
Lo, he is fallen, and around great storms and the outreaching sea !
Therefore, O man, beware and look toward the end of things that be,
The last of sights, the last of days, and no man's life account as gain
Ere the full tale be finished and the darkness find him without pain.*

Hankin was not a poet and did not move upon these emotional planes, but within the limits of his own

* Professor Gilbert Murray's translation. It is a striking commentary upon the common confusion as to the æsthetic meaning of the choric element in drama that in the recent production of *Œdipus Rex* in this country these last lines which, when spoken as Sophocles directed, by the chorus, have an emotional value scarcely to be paralleled in dramatic poetry, were allotted to Œdipus himself, and so deprived of every vestige of significance.

less ambitious design his instinct guided him to a proportion in this matter that was perfectly just, and he helped definitely towards a new understanding of one of the subtlest principles of dramatic form.

The Last of the De Mullins was written in 1907, and was Hankin's last dramatic work save two one-act plays and an unfinished comedy. The sociological problem which is its theme is set out with his customary lucidity and investigated fairly in terms of art and not of propaganda. Great passion in art is always the product of the imagination, and yet it is in this play which is farther away from imagination than any other of his more important efforts, that he approaches most nearly to passion. The reason is that Hankin's imagination being the least developed of his qualities, the problems of reason which he explored depended for their power of moving him deeply upon the directness with which they were stated. The social question of Janet De Mullin is more complete and clearly stated than those of Mrs. Cassilis and Geoffrey, of Lady Denison or Eustace Jackson. However improbable it may be, it is remotely possible that an adjustment of circumstances might show Mrs. Cassilis to be mistaken, Lady Denison to be wise in her charity, and the Jackson compromise to be something other than the best possible solution of the family conflict. This is not to suggest that Hankin should have resolved these plays in any way other than that he chose, but to point out that in each instance it might be urged that he controlled the conduct of his protagonists to certain ends, and that other ends are conceivable. But Janet's attitude and conduct are inevitable, and her decisions are the only ones that we could accept as being possible. And this tightening up of his reasoning faculty served Hankin for the moment in some measure as a substitute for imaginative intensity and brought him near to passion. Janet is the one figure among his men and women of whom we can think as loving passionately and being passionately loved.

The new seriousness of *The Last of the De Mullins* precluded any free exercise of the wit that had been so admirably employed in the earlier plays, but otherwise his qualities here reach their full maturity. The mastery of style has developed, and the characterisation has gained in subtlety and the power of suggestion. Mrs. De Mullin may be set beside Lady Denison and Mrs. Jackson, and De Mullin himself, choleric and stiff-necked as he is, bears witness anew to the tenderness with which his creator contemplated the foibles and prejudices of his creations. It was a rare gift of Hankin's, one that has been memorable in many greater men, this faculty of making human weakness at least not contemptible. There is scarcely a noble figure in his plays—even Violet Jackson lacks something of courage—and yet there is scarcely one for whom we cannot spare some affection. Lady Faringford herself might discover a heart at any moment.

The two one-act plays, *The Burglar Who Failed* and *The Constant Lover*, were both written in 1908. The former is an amiable little farce, not unpleasing, but far from showing the dramatist at his best. It has an air of being manufactured. But *The Constant Lover* is one of the most perfectly polished excursions in prose comedy dialogue that the new drama has produced. Conceived with a fancy of quite uncommon delicacy, the play is carried through from the first word to the last without a flaw. It is full of good sunshine and laughter, light and debonair yet wholly sincere. Hankin never realised his aim more fully than in this little masterpiece, and although it stands of necessity below his more ambitious work in many ways it is, perhaps, a more perfect achievement than anything else that he did. He himself valued it highly, and the last letter he ever wrote closed with a reference to it, poignant and yet not without cheer.

When he died Hankin left an unfinished play, *Thompson*. He had written the first act and some later fragments. Relying far more upon a conventional and definite plot than was his custom, it was clearly his intention to give free rein in the dialogue to the wit of which he was a master. Mr. George Calderon's able completion of an extremely difficult task must speak for itself. In addition to his plays Hankin wrote a number of essays on the theatre which, apart from the excellence of their matter, are remarkable for their admirable prose. As in the plays, imaginative beauty is beyond the writer's aim, but there is always a clear-cut precision, a lucidity and balance of statement, that are a lasting delight even when the subject under discussion is not of permanent interest or the point of view has become obsolete.

But when the Puritan stayed away from the theatre altogether, irrespective of the character of the play presented, his approval or disapproval became a matter of indifference to the management.

Introduction

It is very gratifying, of course, when you put up a play to have it praised by the godly for its elevating tendency. But if none of the godly will come to see it your only course is to withdraw it and substitute something to attract the wicked. For the wicked, with all their faults, buy seats. And so the drama, which, like the rest of the arts, is in its essence neither moral nor immoral, neither religious nor irreligious, got a bad name, and when a calling, or an art, or an institution gets a bad name it soon begins to deserve it.

That is a fair example of the style employed in these essays, and it would be difficult to find a higher excellence in the same province.

In these occasional papers Hankin makes many shrewd observations upon his art and allows us many entertaining glimpses of his philosophy in the rough, of the materials in his workshop. How suggestive, for example, in the light of the plays, is that passage in the essay on " Mr. Bernard Shaw as Critic," where he slyly opposes his own spirit of comedy to the rather strait solemnity that he was one of the few men wise enough to find in his subject. Quoting a paragraph from Mr. Shaw's " Dramatic Opinions," he comments, " This is not the voice of a jester. It is the voice of Dr. Clifford," and proceeds,

Again, of Miss Mary Anderson's autobiography he writes :

" Note how she assumes, this girl who thinks she has been an artist, that the object of going on the stage is to sparkle in the world and that the object of life is happiness ! "

One can almost hear the thump on the cushion as the preacher utters that sentence. Yet I fancy most people have been in the habit of regarding Mr. Shaw's attitude towards the theatre as one of flippant tolerance largely tinged with contempt. The republication of these criticisms should serve to correct that impression. One would rather like to hear, by the way, what the " object of life " really is from Mr. Shaw's point of view. Perhaps some day he will write a play about it.

26

Introduction

St. John Hankin lived and wrote at the beginning of a new movement, and his permanent distinction in drama will be rather that of right endeavour and the recapture of just instincts than of full-bodied achievement. But that his plays have durable qualities there is no question. They are a valuable effort towards the re-establishment of the union between drama and literature; they contain at least a suggestion of a return to true principles of dramatic form; they have not style in its rarer manifestation, but they have style, and that is much. Hankin's characters are not very passionately conceived, nor are they stirred often by the essential emotions of men, but they have life. The comedy which is Falstaff can stale only with the change of fundamental humanity: the comedy which is Eustace Jackson might lose some of its flavour with a change of certain social conditions; Eustace is, nevertheless, a quick creation and not a puppet. The *Note on Happy Endings* pleasantly emphasises the fine objectivity with which the dramatist saw his characters. In bringing them into existence he gave them also some independence of being, and is able seriously to discuss their future and their problems of conduct with as much detachment as he would gossip of his neighbours over the teacups. In the essay on Mr. Shaw he gives counsel to critics that is peculiarly valuable in the consideration of his own plays:

Our dramatic critics, as a class, are always asking whether the dramatist is doing what *they* want, instead of giving their minds to the only question of any importance critically, namely, whether he has done what *he* wants, and done it competently.

And done it competently. That is the point. It does not follow that even if he has done this we shall like his work, but in that event it is better to leave it alone than to denounce it for not being something else. Swinburne was not far wide of the mark when he said that the only criticism of value was the criticism that praised. Those of us who believe that the stage cannot regain its full vigour until it has rediscovered poetry as its natural expression, find in Hankin and his three or four adventurous fellows invigorating promise rather than fulfilment, but we are foolish if we refuse gratitude to the men who have made the first step towards the new estate and deny ourselves the pleasure that their work can give. Among these men Hankin takes an honourable place, and that he was one of the few who first sought to bring back sincerity and a fit dignity of form to a great art is a distinction of which he will not easily be deprived.

JOHN DRINKWATER.

August 1912.

THE TWO MR. WETHERBYS

A MIDDLE-CLASS COMEDY IN THREE ACTS

" Life is a comedy to those who think,
a tragedy to those who feel."

HORACE WALPOLE

SCENES

Act   I.   *The Drawing-room at the James Wetherbys'.*

Act II.   *The Dining-room at the James Wetherbys'.*

Act III.   *Same as Act I.*

The curtain is dropped for a moment half-way through Act II to represent the lapse of three hours.

CHARACTERS

RICHARD WETHERBY, *the bad Mr. Wetherby, living in a bachelor flat in London.*

CONSTANTIA, *Margaret's sister, married to Richard but separated from him.*

JAMES WETHERBY, *the good Mr. Wetherby, living* en famille *at Norwood.*

MARGARET, *his wife.*

AUNT CLARA, *aunt to Margaret and Constantia, a pious old lady of sixty-five.*

ROBERT CARNE, *her nephew, a solemn prig with no digestion.*

MAID *at the James Wetherbys'.*

SCENE: Mr. James Wetherby's house at Norwood. The action of the play takes some twenty hours, from the afternoon of one day to the forenoon of the next.

THE TWO MR. WETHERBYS

ACT I

SCENE.—*The* JAMES WETHERBYS' *drawing-room at Norwood. A door on the right leads to Hall. French windows at back, closed, give on to suburban garden. Fireplace on the left, writing-table with chair, facing audience. Circular settee to seat three, one with back to audience, the other two facing right and left, occupies centre of stage. General furnishing of room philistine but not shabby. A profusion of plush photograph frames on mantelpiece and on upright piano which stands against wall on the right. One of the most conspicuous frames on mantelpiece contains photograph of* JAMES WETHERBY.

When Curtain rises, AUNT CLARA, *an old lady of sixty-five, is discovered in arm-chair making a crochet shawl.* JAMES *is sitting near her on settee reading a newspaper aloud.*

JAMES [*in bored voice*]. "It is, however, abundantly clear that the Government possesses the confidence of the country and that unless some unforeseen difficulty arises, the present administration will remain in power at least until the autumn." [*Yawns slightly.*] I beg your pardon, Aunt Clara. "Meantime it is for the Prime Minister and his

colleagues to take measures to prevent any diminu-
tion in that confidence, and to see to it that when
the next General Election takes place, the Conservative party are not merely returned to power,
but returned with an even larger majority. Only
in this way can the enemies of this country be
convinced that her destiny is in strong and capable
hands, and be restrained from embarking on enter-
prises hurtful to her interests or damaging to her
prestige." [*Yawns.*] "To hand over the task of
forming a Government to the disunited factions of
the Opposition would be——"

AUNT CLARA [*in hard clear tone*]. Will you kindly
pick up my wool, James? It has rolled under the
settee.

JAMES. Certainly, Aunt Clara. [*Grovels for it,
and after disentangling it from various chair legs,
returns with it triumphant, but flushed with exertion.*]
Here it is. [*Places it on the table beside her. She
replaces it on her lap where it is obvious that it will
once more fall in a minute or two.*] Now where was
I? Ah, here we are. [*Resuming bored voice.*] "It
is however abundantly clear that the Government
possesses the confidence of the country [AUNT
CLARA's *ball again seeks the floor*] and that unless
some unforeseen difficulty arises the present administration will remain in power. . . ."
[*Reads on as before.*

AUNT CLARA [*feeling for wool*]. There! It's gone
again!

JAMES [*bored*]. Where is it *now*, Aunt?

AUNT CLARA. On the floor. I had it on my lap
a moment ago. It must have rolled under that

chair. Will you give it me, please ? [JAMES *puts down paper with the least possible suggestion of irritation and recommences grovelling. Finally again emerges successful and places it on table.*] Thank you, James. [*Replaces it on her lap.*]

JAMES [*eyeing the manœuvre with strong disfavour*]. Wouldn't it be better to leave it on the table ? Then it wouldn't be so likely to slip off.

AUNT CLARA [*placidly*]. No, I'm used to having it on my lap.

JAMES. Very well, Aunt. Shall I go on ? [*Picks up paper again.*] " It is however abundantly clear that the Government possesses the confidence of the country and that unless some unforeseen difficulty arises . . ." [*Yawns again.*]

AUNT CLARA [*in her hard, clear tones*]. Haven't you read that part before ?

JAMES. It does sound rather familiar.

AUNT CLARA [*severely*]. I'm afraid you're not reading with much attention, James.

JAMES. I suppose not, I'm rather tired. [*Smothers another yawn.*]

AUNT CLARA [*offended*]. Perhaps we had better put aside our reading for this afternoon, then.

JAMES [*putting down paper with sigh of relief and rising*]. Very well, Aunt.

[*Strolls towards garden.*

AUNT CLARA [*quite unconscious of this manœuvre*]. We might talk a little instead. After luncheon when I'm not being read to, I like to converse for a few minutes. It prevents me from going to sleep.

JAMES [*to her, turning back from garden*]. You're sure you wouldn't *rather* go to sleep ?

AUNT CLARA. No, James. I do not approve of this modern habit of sleeping during the day. [JAMES *sighs dismally and goes to fire where he stands with back to mantelpiece, looking profoundly bored.*] [*Putting down crochet on table.*] Has Constantia come yet ?

JAMES. No, she won't be here much before tea, I expect.

AUNT CLARA. And Richard ?

JAMES. Dick comes about the same time.

AUNT CLARA [*reproachfully*]. I cannot think how you could have asked Richard to stay here ! After the way he treated Constantia !

JAMES [*casually*]. Oh, Dick's not a bad fellow. He didn't get on with Constantia, of course, but he's got his good points all the same.

AUNT CLARA [*severely*]. I have never been able to find them. His treatment of your sister-in-law was shameful. I am sure with *your* high principles you would be the last to defend it.

JAMES [*hastily*]. Of course, of course. Still one mustn't judge too harshly.

AUNT CLARA. I hope I do not, James. Indeed, it would be hard to do so in *this* case.

JAMES [*bored*]. He's only coming for one night. And after all he is my brother.

AUNT CLARA. *That* scarcely seems to me to be in his favour. You are too forgiving, James. Personally I don't approve of this modern habit of forgiving people. It encourages them. And to invite him here ! What *will* Constantia think ?

JAMES. I did it partly to oblige Constantia. When the separation between her and my brother was decided on, it was arranged that the two parties should meet once a year. It was thought that this might open the way to a reconciliation later. When the date for the meeting approached, the question immediately arose, where should it take place ? Constantia wished it to be at her house here in Norwood. Dick declined this, and suggested his flat in Maddox Street. Each of them, in fact, wanted it to take place on his own ground. To put an end to all discussion I suggested that it should be here. And here it is to be. [*Smothers another yawn.*]

Aunt Clara. Ah, James, you are always thoughtful for others ! If only your brother had been like you ! But he has *no* heart.

James. Dick's all right. He's been a little wild, but he'll settle down. [*Looks at watch.*] I suppose he'll be here about half-past four.

Aunt Clara. Robert will arrive rather earlier.

James [*endeavouring to conceal his disgust*]. Robert ! Why, he was here to luncheon.

Aunt Clara. Yes, but he is coming back to tea. In Constantia's interest he thought as many of her relatives as possible should be present during the interview—to support her.

James [*grimly*]. I don't think *Robert* would be much support.

Aunt Clara. You never can tell. A man of his high principles !

James [*impatiently*]. Oh, his *principles* are all right.

Aunt Clara. I am sure *you* do not undervalue such things.

JAMES [*hastily*]. My dear Aunt Clara, certainly not. Still Robert is not exactly a *strong* man, is he ?—except in principles, I mean.

[*Crosses to the table.*

AUNT CLARA. My poor nephew certainly enjoys wretched health.

JAMES. I wonder whether he has enough to do ?

[*At back of table.*

AUNT CLARA [*complacently*]. Robert has *plenty* of occupation. He comes to see me every day !

JAMES. Yes, he's generally here, I notice.

AUNT CLARA. You are so hospitable. And Robert is devoted to his relations. That shows such a nice nature.

JAMES [*bored*]. No doubt.

AUNT CLARA [*enthusiastically*]. And then he does so much good. Always busy about collecting subscriptions for some deserving object. I call that such a *useful* life. His means, poor fellow, don't allow of his contributing himself, but he collects quite a large sum from *others*.

JAMES [*grimly*]. Yes, I've noticed that !

AUNT CLARA. I am sure you are grateful to him. He is always pointing out to you institutions where money may be safely bestowed. Ill-health, which makes most people selfish, has not been able to spoil *my* nephew.

JAMES. Poor Robert, he is certainly a martyr to indisposition. [*Struck by an idea.*] Do you think, Aunt Clara, that the air of Norwood really agrees with him ?

AUNT CLARA. I have not noticed that his health grows any worse.

JAMES [*eagerly*]. Oh yes, it does. He *pines*, Aunt Clara, positively *pines* for a more bracing air. The East coast, for instance !

AUNT CLARA. Ah, James, always considerate. [*Complacently.*] But Robert will never go anywhere where he cannot constantly come and see me. *That* I am sure of. Indeed, it would not be good for him, he has so few distractions.

JAMES [*depressed*]. That's true. [*Walks down and turns, brightening again.*] But why shouldn't you go, too, Aunt Clara ? I'm sure it can't be a good thing for *you* to remain in one place for so long together. Don't you think a change would do *you* good ?

AUNT CLARA [*virtuously*]. I was never a gadabout. And I disapprove of this modern mania for change. Besides with only my little annuity——

JAMES [*interrupting eagerly*]. Yes, yes, I know. [*Crosses to left of* AUNT CLARA.] But for Robert's sake ? You might take him with you, and of course I should be delighted to contribute——

AUNT CLARA [*patting his shoulder affectionately*]. No, no, James. Your heart is ever generous, but in this case there is really no necessity. The air here suits me excellently, and Robert is quite as well as can be expected. Besides there is Margaret to be thought of. I could not leave *her* !

JAMES. I'll look after Margaret.

AUNT CLARA. I am sure you would. I know how devoted you are to her. But Margaret likes to have her own family about her.

JAMES [*ruefully*]. So she does.
     [*Crosses to writing-table and sits down.*

The Two Mr. Wetherbys

AUNT CLARA [*affectionately*]. So you mustn't thin *any* more about this. It was generous of you to propose it, but I am *quite* contented here. Living in your house, James, with Robert and Constantia coming in *every* day, I have everything that I need for happiness. [*Wipes tear from her eye.*] Ah, here is Robert.

Enter ROBERT, *a cadaverous shambling man of five and thirty.*

ROBERT [*nods to* JAMES]. Good morning, Aunt Clara. You weren't down for lunch.

AUNT CLARA. No, I had a little soup in my room. I had a bad night.

ROBERT [*sitting on settee, gloomily*]. Ah, *my* insomnia is chronic.

AUNT CLARA [*bravely*]. But we must not complain. On the whole my health is wonderfully good.

ROBERT. I wish I could say that. After the Otaheite mission meeting last night I felt positively faint.

AUNT CLARA. Did you see James ?

ROBERT. No, was he there ?

AUNT CLARA. Of course. You know his interest in Otaheite.

JAMES [*hastily*]. Oh, in a large meeting like that it is so easy to miss a face.

ROBERT [*in a hard voice*]. I shouldn't have called it a large meeting.

JAMES [*hurriedly*]. Relatively large ! Of course it wasn't *crowded.*

ROBERT. I should think not. Why, there were scarcely a hundred people there.

JAMES [*judicially*]. Indeed? I should have thought more than a *hundred*. [*To* AUNT CLARA, *with rapid change of subject*.] Shall I begin to read to you again, Aunt Clara?

AUNT CLARA. Not now, thank you, it is almost time for my walk.

ROBERT. By the way, James, I have here an appeal for a good object which may well claim your support. The Mahommedan Conversion Fund. A most deserving field.

JAMES [*irritably*]. Oh, come, I hardly think we need go as far as the Mahommedans to find a deserving object.

ROBERT. I don't see that. After all Arabia is nearer than Otaheite.

JAMES [*indifferently*]. I dare say.

ROBERT. And as you took the trouble to go to the meeting last night—I can't think how I came to miss you there; by the by, where were you sitting?—I should have thought——

JAMES [*rising hastily and going over to him*]. My dear fellow, you're quite right. Converting the Mahommedans is a most useful field. Leave me that paper and I'll look through it.

[*Takes paper and turns away.*

Enter MARGARET *with* AUNT CLARA'S *bonnet and shawl.*

Hullo, Maggie. Been lying down? [*Kisses her.*]

MARGARET. For half an hour. The sun is shining brightly now, Aunt Clara. Hadn't you better have your walk?

AUNT CLARA. I hardly feel up to it.

The Two Mr. Wetherbys

JAMES [*going up to her chair*]. Oh yes, I really think you should, just a turn or two in the garden. [*Helps her to rise.*

AUNT CLARA. Very well, perhaps a few steps. [*Is helped into bonnet and shawl.*] And which of my dear nephews shall escort me ? [*Beaming.*] James, I think.

JAMES [*hastily*]. No, no, Aunt. Robert shall go with you while I look through this Mahommedan Appeal.

AUNT CLARA [*much touched at this fresh evidence of self-denial*]. Ah, James, always willing to deny yourself. Come, Robert.

ROBERT [*rising heavily*]. Very well. Perhaps a gentle walk will do me good. [*Exit* AUNT CLARA *to garden supported by* ROBERT.]

[MARGARET *escorts both as far as window.* JAMES *with a sigh of relief goes to writing-table with Mahommedan Appeal, eyes it with strong disfavour, glances at a page or two, then with a wry face takes out cheque book and writes cheque.* MARGARET *returning from window goes to him, and noticing his depression, lays hand on shoulder.*

MARGARET. Tired, dear ?

JAMES. A little.

[*There is a pause, during which* MARGARET *pats* JAMES *affectionately on shoulder while he fidgets with paper-knife.*

JAMES [*diffidently*]. Don't you think, Maggie, that Aunt Clara might *sometimes* go and stay with some one else ?

MARGARET [*puzzled*]. Whom can she stay with ?

JAMES [*hopelessly*]. That's just it, whom indeed !

MARGARET. You see she *has* no one except us—and Constantia.

JAMES. That wouldn't be much change for her! Constantia's always here anyhow.

MARGARET [*gently*]. Not much change certainly.

[*There is another perceptible pause.*

JAMES [*with an effort*]. Well then, Robert? Don't you think he might come *rather* less frequently?

MARGARET. My dear! He only comes to luncheon occasionally.

JAMES. Half a dozen times a week.

MARGARET. No, no, James, only three or four.

JAMES. Is that all? It seems oftener!

MARGARET [*kneels by him, fondling his hair*]. What's the matter with you, dear? You seem out of spirits.

JAMES [*taking her hand and pressing it*]. It's nothing. Only we never seem to get any time to ourselves, do we?

MARGARET. Not very much, perhaps.

JAMES. And it would certainly be more comfortable if we did, eh, little girl?

[*Looking up at her face.*

MARGARET [*gently*]. But we mustn't think only of *comfort*, must we?

JAMES. What an angel you are!

[*Takes her hand and kisses it.*

Enter SERVANT.

SERVANT. Mrs. Richard Wetherby.

JAMES. Confound!

Enter Constantia, *an imposing figure, handsomely dressed in black, rather as if she had gone into half mourning to mark her sense of her separation from her husband.*

Margaret [*putting hand over his mouth*]. Hush! [*Rises to greet her sister.*] Good afternoon, Connie. [*Kisses her.*]

[*They meet.* Constantia *crosses to* James *after kissing* Margaret.

James [*rising*]. How are you?

Constantia [*in her elaborate manner*]. Thank you, James, I am tolerably well. Has Richard arrived yet?

James. Not yet.

Constantia. I am glad of that. I would rather be here to receive him. I shall feel more *at home*.

[James *makes a face, which* Margaret *observes, and turns towards garden window.*

Margaret. Aunt Clara is in the garden.

James [*hurriedly*]. Yes. She has just gone out with Robert. [*Insinuatingly.*] Oughtn't you to go and say " How do you do " to her?

Constantia. Very well. Perhaps I had better do so. I shall not be long.

James [*as soon as she is out of the room*]. Pray don't hurry. [*Exit* Constantia *to garden. There is a third significant pause during which* Margaret *crosses to settee.* James *comes to her, repossesses himself of her hand, and quietly sits by her side.*] [*Reflectively.*] I suppose it wouldn't be possible to get Constantia to *move*, would it?

Margaret. Move?

James. Yes, go away from Norwood altogether.

MARGARET. Oh no, she likes being near us.

JAMES [*gloomily*]. I was afraid so.

MARGARET [*kissing him*]. How silly you are this afternoon. I've never seen you like this before. Why shouldn't Connie live near us ?

JAMES [*petulantly*]. Why *should* she ? Why doesn't she go and live with her husband like other women ?

MARGARET. With Richard ? But you know her principles.

JAMES [*bored*]. Here's another of them.

MARGARET [*not understanding*]. What, dear ?

JAMES [*recovering himself*]. Nothing. Only I seem to have heard rather a lot about principles to-day.

MARGARET. As a member of the Married Woman's Protection League, Constantia naturally has a high ideal of a husband's duty to his wife. A very high ideal. So has Aunt Clara. So has Robert.

JAMES. They're a remarkably unanimous family.

MARGARET. Constantia would have considered it *wrong* to condone Richard's infidelity.

JAMES. There was no proof that Dick was unfaithful.

MARGARET. What other explanation could there be of his late hours, his constant absences from home ?

JAMES. Was he ever asked to explain them ?

MARGARET. Of course. Constantia *never* allowed Richard to be out after midnight without demanding an explanation. She felt it to be her duty.

JAMES. What did Dick say ?

MARGARET. He *laughed* at her. [JAMES *shows a*

tendency to laugh also.] Jim! I believe you're laughing too!

JAMES. Well, the interviews must have been rather comic. Constantia proclaiming the rights of women and the wickedness of husbands, and old Dick grinning away on the hearthrug.

[*Begins to laugh again.*

MARGARET [*shocked*]. Oh, Jim! I never thought you would make a joke of such a thing.

JAMES [*pulling himself up*]. No! No! Dick didn't behave at all well. Still I think Constantia might have managed him better.

MARGARET. Constantia never attempted to *manage* her husband. She had too much sense of her own dignity. She merely insisted upon her rights.

JAMES. Rather a maddening attitude that?

MARGARET. Richard was in fault.

JAMES. Perhaps there were faults on Constantia's side as well.

MARGARET [*pained*]. Oh, Jim, I thought you never judged people harshly.

JAMES. No, no, dear. You misunderstand me. I only mean that perhaps Constantia did not show Dick much affection. She's not what you would call a demonstrative woman.

MARGARET [*gently*]. I don't think she ever failed in her duty.

JAMES. A woman must do a lot more than her duty if she's to make her husband happy.

MARGARET. Richard did not make her happy either, you know.

JAMES. That's it, you see! They're quits.

MARGARET [*affectionately*]. It's like you, dear, to try and defend Richard. You always make the best of everybody. Still he was greatly to blame.

JAMES. I'm afraid he was. [*Slight pause.*] But you won't do anything to prevent a reconciliation, will you ?

MARGARET. No. But you mustn't ask me to encourage it.

JAMES [*rises and comes forward*]. Well, let's hope they'll patch it up between them to-day. She's not seen Dick for a year. And she must have been fond of him once.

MARGARET. What does Robert think ?

JAMES [*hastily*]. Oh, I don't think we need consult Robert.

MARGARET. By the way, Robert and I are going to the great meeting at Lambeth to-night in aid of the Bishop's Sustentation Fund. We shall dine in town. You don't mind ?

JAMES. What about Dick ? He'll be here.

MARGARET. It is because of Richard that I am going. I was afraid it might seem rather marked if I were out the only night he's dining here, but what was I to do ?

JAMES [*briefly*]. Not go, I suppose.

MARGARET. I couldn't do that. Of course, I don't want to hurt Richard's feelings, but I would rather not sit at table with a man who is living apart from his wife.

JAMES. I should have thought it was no worse to sit at table with a man who is separated from his wife than with a wife who is separated from her husband. Constantia is here often enough !

MARGARET [*slightly scandalised*]. The cases are hardly parallel.

JAMES. I should think they weren't ! Considering that your sister is here all day and every day, I think you might manage to meet my brother at dinner once a year.

MARGARET [*pause, rises*]. I'm sorry you're vexed, dear. I hoped you wouldn't mind. [*Pause.*] However, it doesn't matter. I'll tell Robert I've changed my plans, and he and I will both have dinner with you here before the meeting.

JAMES. Heaven forbid ! Robert was here at luncheon. He will be here to tea. I'm hanged if he shall dine here as well !

MARGARET. Well, dear, what can I do ? I can't very well disappoint Robert. It would be unkind.

JAMES [*remorsefully*]. What a brute I am ! [*Kisses her.*] Of course you mustn't. Dine in town by all means. I'll make your excuses to Dick, and we'll go round to the club after dinner and play billiards. There, dear, I'm sorry I was cross. I suppose I'm out of sorts or something.

[*Crosses to table.*

MARGARET [*crosses to* JAMES *and caresses him*]. Poor Jim ! You won't mind dining alone with him, will you ?

JAMES. Of course not, he won't eat me. Besides I shall have Aunt Clara.

MARGARET. Yes, I was forgetting Aunt Clara.

JAMES. Happy woman !   [*Sits.*

MARGARET [*laughing*]. You're evidently not well at all. I shall send for Dr. Long, and he'll give you some horrid medicine.   That Otaheite meeting was over ever so late last night.   I expect that tired you.   [*They embrace.*

Enter by window CONSTANTIA, AUNT CLARA *and*
   ROBERT.   ROBERT *enters behind* AUNT CLARA, *who
   leans on* CONSTANTIA'S *left arm.   He stands by
   the window gloomily observing the embrace, then
   turns away.*   MARGARET *moves the arm-chair a
   little.*   CONSTANTIA, *after depositing* AUNT CLARA,
   comes to the settee.   MARGARET *goes to the window.*

JAMES [*ruefully*]. Interrupted again !
                           [*Rises, and crosses the room.*
   [CONSTANTIA *seats herself on settee.*   AUNT CLARA *is
in arm-chair.   The latter resumes her crochet,* ROBERT
moons about.
   ROBERT [*looking at watch*]. Half-past four. Time
for tea.
   JAMES. Dick will be here directly.
   ROBERT [*unctuously*]. I'm afraid this will be a very
painful meeting for all of us.
   JAMES. That reminds me.   I expect, Constantia,
you'd rather have your interview with Richard in
private ? [*to* CONSTANTIA, *standing between her and*
ROBERT.]
   ROBERT [*interrupting*]. I hardly think——
 . JAMES. My dear Robert, will you kindly allow
Constantia to decide for herself ?   [*To* CONSTANTIA]
Well ?
   CONSTANTIA. Thank you, James, I think that will
certainly be the best arrangement.
   JAMES. Very well, then.   [*Crosses to fireplace and*

stands back to fire—rings bell.] Jane shall show Dick into the library. Margaret and I will go there and give him some tea. You, Aunt Clara and Robert will have tea here. After tea I will bring Dick here and leave you to have your talk with him in private.

Enter MAID.

When Mr. Richard comes show him into the library, and let me know.

MAID. Very well, sir.   [*Exit.*

ROBERT. You are sure you would not rather have some one at hand ?

CONSTANTIA. Pray do not be ridiculous, Robert. I trust I am able to conduct an interview with my husband without outside assistance.

JAMES. Of course ! And I hope the result will be to bring you together again.

[CONSTANTIA *bows coldly.*

AUNT CLARA. James !

JAMES [*hastily*]. That is, of course, if you are conscientiously able to forgive him.

ROBERT [*rises—grunts*]. By the way, James, about that Mahommedan Appeal——

JAMES [*impatiently*]. Oh yes, I've looked through it. There's a cheque in my pocket somewhere. Here it is.   [*Hands it to him.*

ROBERT [*sitting, after examining the amount*]. Thank you, James. I felt sure the good work would find a supporter in you.

JAMES. Yes, yes, of course. Always glad to do what I can. [*The front door bell rings.*] Ah, that must be Dick. Ready, Maggie ? [*To* CONSTANTIA]

Then you will see Dick alone here in say ten minutes.

MAID enters.

MAID. Mr. Richard is in the library, sir.

JAMES. Very well. Take him some tea and bring some here. Come, Maggie.

[Exeunt MARGARET and JAMES.

AUNT CLARA [seated by fireplace]. It must be very painful for dear James to meet his brother in these distressing circumstances. If only Richard were more like him. But the two brothers are quite different ! [Shakes her head mournfully.

ROBERT. Richard is by nature incurably frivolous and vicious.

CONSTANTIA [calmly]. I do not think anything is to be gained by exaggerating my husband's failings.

Enter JANE with tea. Moves table a little, puts down tea-tray, and brings down chair and puts it behind table.

There was always a regrettable levity about his behaviour which showed a tendency to increase with years. And, of course, his moral character is scandalous. [Goes over to tea-table.] But, these defects are not necessarily incurable. Tea, Aunt Clara ?

AUNT CLARA. Thank you.

CONSTANTIA. Take this to Aunt Clara, Robert.

[ROBERT rises heavily from chair, gets tea and crosses to AUNT CLARA.

AUNT CLARA. I am afraid Richard's disposition always lacked the note of seriousness which is so beautiful in James. [*Takes tea*]—Thank you, Robert—I remember people used to joke about it. They called Richard " The bad Mr. Wetherby " and James " The good Mr. Wetherby."

[ROBERT *stands by arm-chair.*

CONSTANTIA. I remember. However, our separation will have sobered him, no doubt.

[*Gives* ROBERT *his tea.*

AUNT CLARA. Let us hope so, my dear.

ROBERT [*taking bread-and-butter.*] Have you made up your mind what attitude to adopt towards him? If I might advise I should urge that you receive his advances with the utmost reserve.

[*Sits down on settee.*

AUNT CLARA. Yes, Robert is right. Do not allow your heart to betray you into any course which your reason would not approve.

CONSTANTIA [*calmly helping herself to cake*]. I think you may count on me not to err in *that* direction.

AUNT CLARA. I am glad to hear it. Modern wives are far too ready to forgive their husbands. It is the cause of many unhappy homes.

CONSTANTIA [*calmly*]. I did not say I shall *not* forgive Richard.

AUNT CLARA. My dear !

CONSTANTIA. On the contrary. It is my intention to forgive him this afternoon, after he has duly expressed contrition and asked for forgiveness.

AUNT CLARA. But can you be sure that his repentance is sincere ?

CONSTANTIA [*philosophically*]. Of course there can be no certainty in these things. But I see every reason why it should be. He must have felt our separation acutely. In the early days of our marriage Richard was by no means without tenderness.

ROBERT [*in a hollow voice*]. Constantia, is this wise ?   [*He takes bread-and-butter.*

CONSTANTIA. I think so. After all, Richard is my husband. And I have not found my position since I decided to live apart from him altogether an agreeable one. Socially indeed it has great inconveniences. [*Rises and takes* AUNT CLARA'S *cup and places it on tray—seating herself again.*] More tea, Aunt ?

AUNT CLARA [*making gesture of dissent*]. Well, my dear, of course you must do what your *conscience* tells you to be right.

CONSTANTIA. Exactly. I shall not pardon him too quickly. I shall just yield gradually to his protestations. [*Eats some cake delicately.*] After all, a year is a long time and it is better to err on the side of leniency. [*Pours herself out more tea.*] A year ago, I felt obliged to leave Richard—I could not endure his heartless behaviour. Indeed a wife who condones her husband's irregularities is wanting in her duty. And at the time I intended never to return to him. But one must not be vindictive. And the position of a woman who is separated from her husband is not a comfortable one. It has all the disadvantages of widowhood without its compensations. Yes, on the whole I think Richard has been punished long enough. More tea, Robert ?

ROBERT [*rising, and bringing his cup*]. I fear you

are leaning unduly towards mercy. [*Pause.*] I greatly fear it.

[CONSTANTIA *pours out* ROBERT'S *tea. He takes it and sits down again, taking bread-and-butter.*

CONSTANTIA. I am willing to take the risk. At least I shall feel that I have done what is right in forgiving my husband. Besides there are practical matters to be considered, the loss of income and so forth. When I left Richard I had to move into a smaller house and make other heavy sacrifices. The allowance he makes me, though sufficient, is considerably smaller than the income I enjoyed as his wife.

AUNT CLARA. I don't think you must allow that to weigh with you. After all what is money ?

ROBERT [*unctuously*]. What indeed !

[*He takes more bread-and-butter.*

CONSTANTIA [*frigidly*]. My dear Robert, of course I am above all *sordid* considerations in this matter. I shall do what I consider right in any circumstances. But there is no use in shutting one's eyes to things.

AUNT CLARA [*dismally*]. Well, well, my dear, I trust you will not find you have made a mistake.

CONSTANTIA [*coldly*]. I do not usually make mistakes, I believe. I shall forgive Richard this afternoon after he has expressed his regret in suitable terms. Of course I shall speak to him very seriously and caution him as to his future conduct. But afterwards I shall forgive him.

Enter MARGARET.

MARGARET [*at door*]. Richard will come to you now, Connie, if you are ready to see him.

CONSTANTIA. Very well.

[*Pours herself out some tea.*

MARGARET [*going to* AUNT CLARA *and helping her to rise*]. Come, Aunt Clara. Let me take you to your room. [*To* ROBERT.] I think you had better go now, Robert.

ROBERT. Certainly. [*Putting cup on chiffonier and finishing bread-and-butter.*]

[*Exit* ROBERT *sulkily.*

MARGARET [*at door*]. Jim will bring Richard to you in a minute or two.

[*Exit with* AUNT CLARA.

[CONSTANTIA *puts down her cup directly they leave, rises, but hearing voices, sits on settee. There is an appreciable pause. Then enter* JAMES *and* DICK. *The latter is a handsome, careless, jovial-looking man of five-and-thirty, very cheerful and quite at his ease.*

DICK [*going up to* CONSTANTIA *and shaking hands*]. How do you do, Con? Pretty well, I hope?

CONSTANTIA. Thank you. I am quite well.

DICK [*cheerfully*]. That's right.

JAMES [*at door*]. Now I'll leave you two together. You may have things to talk of alone.

[*Going.*

DICK. Not at all, my dear fellow. Stay by all means. Con and I have no secrets.

JAMES [*awkwardly*]. But I think——

[*Going again.*

DICK. Nonsense, Jim. Sit down. What on earth *should* we have to talk about? Don't be absurd.

ACT I   55

JAMES [*still going*]. Oh, but—Constantia said she would prefer to speak to you alone.

DICK. Ah, that's different. If Con has anything private to say to me I'm agreeable. I always am. Off with you. I say, what time's dinner ?

[*Goes up to* JAMES.

JAMES. Seven. By the way, Margaret asks you to excuse her. She has to dine out.

DICK. All right. [*Nods cheerily to* JAMES, *who goes out.*] Well, Con, what have you got to say to *me*, ch ?

CONSTANTIA [*with dignity*]. Have *you* nothing to say to *me*, Richard ?

DICK. I think not. Nothing special.

CONSTANTIA. Then I hardly see the object of this meeting.

DICK [*cheerily*]. Nor do I. But *you* arranged it, you know.

CONSTANTIA [*stiffly*]. Pardon me !

DICK. No ? Ah yes, I remember. You suggested every six months. I thought once a year quite sufficient. You see I was right.

[*Crosses behind settee.*

CONSTANTIA [*majestically*]. This is not an occasion for levity.

DICK. My remark was not intentionally humorous.

[*There is a pause during which* CONSTANTIA *shows signs of impatience.* DICK, *quite at his ease, strolls over to fire and warms himself. Presently he takes up framed photograph of* JAMES *which stands conspicuously on mantelpiece.*]

I say, what a beastly picture of old Jim ! Don't you think so ? [*Holds it up.*

CONSTANTIA [*icily*]. It seems to me a satisfactory likeness.

DICK. No, it's so smug and solemn. Poor old chap, I expect he has a pretty boring time of it down here, eh ?

CONSTANTIA [*with elaborate sarcasm*]. I have not heard him complain.

DICK. I dare say not. He's a patient sort of chap is old Jim. [*Shakes his head at photograph as he puts it back on mantelpiece. Then seats himself in arm-chair. There is another awkward pause.*

DICK. By the way, do you still like living in Norwood, Con ? *Ghastly* sort of place I used to think it.

CONSTANTIA. It suits me well enough. I like to be near Margaret and James.

DICK. Ah ! Do *they* like that ?

CONSTANTIA. Certainly.

DICK. Oh ! [*A pause.*] You're tolerably contented then, take it all together ?

[CONSTANTIA *bows*]

That's right. So am I.

CONSTANTIA. Of course a wife who is separated from her husband can never be very happy.

DICK. No doubt. But a husband who isn't separated from his wife can be tolerably miserable too.

CONSTANTIA. Yes, marriage is a tragedy.

DICK. Just so, with comic relief.

CONSTANTIA [*impatiently*]. Pray be serious.

DICK. My dear Con, I *never* am serious. Why on earth should I be ?

ACT I. 57

CONSTANTIA. Don't you understand that by adopting this frivolous tone you are letting a golden opportunity slip ?

DICK. No. Hang me if I do.

CONSTANTIA [*rising with dignity*]. Then no good can come of our continuing this interview.

DICK [*rising also*]. Of course not. What did you expect ?

CONSTANTIA [*exasperated*]. I expected that you would at least have seen the propriety of expressing regret for your past conduct and promising amendment in the future.

DICK. What would have been the use of that ?

CONSTANTIA [*bitterly*]. Oh, nothing. Nothing that interests you at all, I suppose. Only it might have led to a reconciliation between us.

DICK [*by fire, raising his eyebrows*]. I see. [*Deliberately*]. I confess that possibility had *not* occurred to me !

CONSTANTIA [*stiffly*]. Indeed !

DICK [*politely*]. Still it's very good of you to suggest it.

CONSTANTIA [*turning hotly*]. I did *not* suggest it.

DICK. Oh ! I thought you did.

CONSTANTIA [*angrily*]. What I said was that had *you* suggested it——

DICK. Yes, yes, of course. What I should have said was it would have been very good of *me* to suggest it. No, that's not right either. Still I appreciate the generosity of your offer.

The Two Mr. Wetherbys

CONSTANTIA [*crossly*]. I made no offer.

DICK. Dear me, I'm afraid I express myself very clumsily.

CONSTANTIA [*savagely*]. You certainly do.

[*Sits on settee.*

DICK [*crosses near settee. Blandly*]. You must put it down to excess of emotion. When a man has been separated from his wife for a year, and there is a suggestion—if that is the right word—that she *might* return to his roof he naturally feels it acutely. The *affection* implied in such a proposal—no, not proposal, hypothesis—is very moving.

CONSTANTIA. I said nothing about affection.

DICK. But it was surely implied ?

CONSTANTIA [*sternly*]. No, Richard. Please understand that my—— [*Pauses for word.*

DICK [*sweetly*]. Mention ?

CONSTANTIA.—my mention of a reconciliation was in no way due to affection. Had I returned to you it would have been solely because I considered it my *duty*.

DICK [*insinuatingly*]. Is that *quite* a satisfactory foundation for domestic happiness ?

CONSTANTIA [*impatiently*]. I was not thinking of *happiness*. [*There is a pause.*

DICK [*calmly*]. Well, Con, I won't ask you to make such a sacrifice.

CONSTANTIA [*virtuously*]. I don't mind sacrificing myself.

DICK [*quietly*]. Ah ! *I* do !

CONSTANTIA [*rising angrily*]. Then there's nothing more to be said.

DICK [*holding out hand*]. Except " good-bye," Con—till next year.

[CONSTANTIA *refuses hand and sweeps out with dignity. DICK stands looking after her with a grim smile. The front door closes sharply.*

CURTAIN

ACT II

SCENE.—*The Dining-room at the* JAMES WETHERBYS'. *Dinner is half over. At the table in the middle of stage are* AUNT CLARA, *facing audience,* JAMES *at one end,* DICK *at the other. The side of table next the audience is empty. The room is the conventional suburban dining-room; windows curtained behind* AUNT CLARA, *sideboard behind* DICK, *fireplace flanked by two leather easy chairs behind* JAMES. *Door on the left.*

Pause. The MAID *hands two sweets.* JAMES, *who looks bored and ill, helps* AUNT CLARA *to jelly.* DICK *helps himself.* JAMES *refuses.*

DICK. My dear chap, you eat nothing. [*Attacks jelly on his plate.*] Does he, Aunt Clara?

AUNT CLARA [*coldly*]. James has never a large appetite.

JAMES. I'm not hungry to-night.

DICK. That's bad. [*Filling his mouth.*] There's nothing like *eating!* It helps a man through life wonderfully.

JAMES. No doubt.

DICK. In fact it's very morbid not to eat. It's not at all a thing to give way to. [*To* MAID.] Bring me some more of that. [*Helps himself.*

JAMES. My dear Dick, what nonsense you talk.

DICK. I dare say. If *you* talked more nonsense

you wouldn't look so beastly seedy. Eh, Aunt Clara ? [*Attacks food.*

AUNT CLARA [*coldly*]. I had not noticed that James was looking unwell.

DICK. He does though. And he looks beastly *serious* too. That's bad. A man should never be serious at meals. Indeed I'm not sure he should ever be serious at all.

[MAID *takes* JAMES'S *and* AUNT CLARA'S *sweet plates and puts two cheese plates.*]

AUNT CLARA. Really, Richard ! Considering the solemn cause which brought you here to-day——

DICK. Yes, Constantia *is* solemn, isn't she ? That's why we didn't get on.

[MAID *changes plates during this scene, afterwards hands biscuits and cheese.*]

AUNT CLARA [*severely*]. It is a pity you are not more like her.

[MAID *gives* DICK *cheese plate.*]

DICK. That's what I never can understand about you solemn people. You're all propagandists. You're not only as solemn as owls yourselves—you want everybody else to be solemn too.

JAMES. Oh come, *you* were preaching the virtue of talking nonsense just now.

DICK. So I was. But only to you, Jim.
[*Takes cheese, which the other two refuse.*
You see I *like* you. But Aunt Clara doesn't like me. [*To* AUNT CLARA.] Oh no, you don't. So why on

earth she should want to convert me to anything I don't know. [*Eats his cheese and biscuit.*

AUNT CLARA. I do not expect *you* to appreciate my motives.

[DICK *grins.*]

JAMES. Aunt Clara means that you aren't an altruist, Dick.

[MAID *removes plates, brushes cloth and puts on dessert during this scene, then Exit.*

DICK. No, I'm not. But I've got a good temper and a rattling good digestion. That's enough for *me.*

JAMES. Is this the way you used to talk to Constantia ?

DICK. Yes.

JAMES. Then I don't wonder she left you.

[DICK *laughs.*]

AUNT CLARA [*rising*]. I cannot be a witness to any more of this levity.

DICK [*genially*]. Don't go, Aunt Clara. Stay till after dessert.

AUNT CLARA. No, I will not—I never eat dessert at night. James, give me your arm.

[JAMES *and* DICK *both rise.* DICK *opens door.* JAMES *helps* AUNT CLARA *out. When he returns* DICK *is back in his chair, cracking nuts and pouring himself out a glass of port.*

JAMES. What a brute you are, Dick ! You've made Aunt Clara furious.

DICK. Very sorry, my dear chap. I did my best to amuse her.

JAMES [*grimly*]. Well, you didn't succeed.   She's gone straight to bed in a tearing rage.

DICK.   Fiery old lady !   Nuts, Jim ?

JAMES.   No, thanks.

DICK [*taking some more, then looking at* JAMES *keenly but kindly*].   My dear old man, what's the matter ?   You really do look awfully pulled down.

JAMES.   Nothing.   We were rather late last night. Perhaps it's that.

DICK [*laughing softly to himself*].   Yes.   How did you account for the fact *here ?*

JAMES [*with a wry face*].   As usual—Missionary Meeting—I nearly got found out, by the way.

DICK.   How was that ?

JAMES.   That fool Robert.   He was there too. It wasn't a crowded house apparently, and he can't make out how he didn't spot me.

[DICK *laughs more.*]

That's right !   [*With a snarl.*]   *Laugh* away !   I suppose it *is* funny—to you.

DICK.   I should think it was.

JAMES.   It isn't to *me*.   It makes me *sick*.   Fancy a man of my age who has to pretend to his wife that he's been to a cursed missionary meeting because he can't tell her he was amusing himself at your club playing cards.

DICK.   Why didn't you tell her ?

JAMES [*crossly*].   How can I ?   She'd never forgive me.   Margaret's a dear little girl and she's awfully fond of me, but she's tremendously strict in her ideas.   Besides I've got such a confoundedly high character to live up to.   If I were just an ordinary person, I dare say she wouldn't be so much shocked. Margaret's not a fool. But she's got it into her head that I'm a sort of saint, and to please her I've got into the habit of pretending to be one, and now I can't give it up. Was there ever such a beastly tangle ?

DICK. Why not make a clean breast of it ?

JAMES. I can't, I tell you. It would be bad enough merely to have to tell her that I'm not the good young man they all think me down here. But I should have to own that I'd been deceiving her almost ever since our marriage. She'd never be able to respect me again, and I should never be able to respect myself. [*Bitterly.*] Indeed, I can't do that *now*.

DICK. My dear chap, you take the whole thing too seriously.

Door opens—enter MAID.

JAMES. Hush ! here's coffee.

[*Coffee is handed—exit* MAID.

DICK [*reflectively*]. It must be a curious thing being so highly thought of—especially by one's wife !

JAMES [*crossly*]. Well, you needn't *sneer* at it.

DICK. I wasn't. Still it seems odd—to me. What did they think of your asking me down here ?

JAMES. Aunt Clara was rather shocked. But she puts it all down to my high principles.

DICK. How does she manage that ?

JAMES. I'm supposed to be such a thoroughly

saintly character that I can't judge any one harshly. Even a beast like you.

DICK. Ho! Ho!

JAMES. Yes. That's *one* advantage in having a good reputation. Whatever you do, people always attribute it to the loftiest motives. If you ask a fellow who's a bad lot to dinner, it's supposed to be because you've such a forgiving disposition. *You* can't say that!

DICK. I don't want to, my dear fellow. And after all, a bad reputation and a good reputation amount to pretty much the same thing in the end.

JAMES [*disgusted*]. I'm hanged if they do.

DICK. Oh yes. *You* can dine with whom you please because you've such a high character. *I* can dine with whom *I* please because I've no character at all. My position is every bit as good as yours. Indeed, I prefer it.

[*Takes cigar and pushes case across to* JAMES.

JAMES [*shocked*]. Ah, you've no conscience.

DICK. No. Have you a match?

JAMES. Here you are.

[*Gets match-box from mantelpiece.*

DICK. Won't you smoke?

JAMES. No. Margaret doesn't like it.

DICK. Poor chap! [*Lights cigar.*] By the way, don't you find the high moral game rather fatiguing?

JAMES [*sighing*]. Sometimes.

DICK. I thought so. That's why you're looking so fagged.

JAMES [*complainingly*]. And yet I'm not naturally a hypocrite. I'd like to be as straightforward as the day. But circumstances were against me. When

I fell in love with Margaret I really did give up all
the old bachelor ways. She was so good [*enthusiastically*], so wonderfully good and sweet, and I
determined I'd be like her. For a time I *was* like
her. It was uphill work, but I was.

[DICK *grins.*]

What are you *grinning* at ?
DICK. Nothing. Go on.
JAMES. Of course she thought me a perfect saint.
I *was* a perfect saint, in fact. And so we were
married and came to live down here. And after
a time—six months or so—I found I couldn't keep
it up. I wanted amusement. But by that time I
was saddled with my ghastly reputation. And I've
been groaning under it ever since.
DICK. Much better have told her.
JAMES [*irritably, fidgeting with cigar-case which
remains on table all through scene*]. I couldn't.
Margaret believed in me ; so did they all. I
couldn't undeceive them. It would have been
simply brutal.
DICK. So you took to hypocrisy.
JAMES [*savagely*]. Oh well, you needn't get
virtuous over it.
DICK [*calmly*]. Not at all, my dear chap.
JAMES [*grumbling*]. It isn't as if I'd been anything
very bad. I'm not a vicious man. I only wanted
to amuse myself—music-halls, an occasional race
meeting, a game of cards at the club. If she'd only
thought me just an ordinary sort of chap, I'd have
told her fast enough. But with *my* character !
Good Lord !

DICK. You'd much better have adopted my system. [*Rises.*

JAMES [*snappishly*]. *Your* system !

DICK. You needn't sniff at it. It's a lot better than yours.

JAMES. What *is* your system ?

DICK [*getting up from table*]. It's very simple. And it's based upon the easiest of all the virtues—Truth !

JAMES. Pshaw !

DICK. Oh yes, it is. [*Goes over to fire, selects armchair and seats himself lazily.*] I hate pretending things. It's such a *fag*. So I've gone in for perfect frankness. In fact, I may say I've carried frankness to a fine art.

JAMES. What rot !

DICK. 'Tisn't rot at all, my dear chap, and so you'd have found if you'd tried it. Truth's a splendid thing in married life. It keeps a home together wonderfully.

JAMES [*sarcastically*]. You seem to have found it so !

DICK [*easily*]. Oh, it sometimes breaks one up too. But it's awfully useful either way.

JAMES. I'm glad you think so.

DICK. You see, in marriage what one has to aim at is a quiet life. *You* tried to get it by pretending to be as good as Margaret thought you. *That* wasn't very successful. *I* tried to get it by never pretending anything at all. The result has exceeded my most sanguine expectations.

JAMES [*ironically*]. You're easily satisfied.

DICK. That's my beautiful nature ! After I

married Constantia I found she hadn't the same *ideals* as I had, not the same *ideals* at all.

JAMES. *Your* ideals !

DICK. Come, my dear chap, *your* ideals haven't shown up particularly well. As I was saying, Con and I wanted different things. She liked regular hours, church on Sunday, afternoon tea parties, bazaars, that ass Robert and his subscription lists, Aunt Clara and her crochet—by the way, how do *you* like Aunt Clara ?

JAMES. Hang Aunt Clara ! [*Rises irritably and begins to put away decanters into sideboard in a restless manner.*

DICK [*blandly*]. That's exactly what *I* said. Well, I soon realised that either Constantia's view of life must prevail or mine. I rebelled—late hours, golf on Sundays, no tea parties, no bazaars, no Robert, no Aunt Clara. Before long I had established a reputation as a complete libertine and was allowed to do as I pleased.

JAMES. I remember. Your conduct was disgraceful.

DICK. Not at all, my dear fellow. I never did anything bad. I'm no more vicious than you are. My bad reputation is as hollow as your good one. We're both frauds together.

JAMES [*impatiently*]. Anyhow, Constantia believed you were vicious.

DICK. Yes. That was part of my system. In this world, Jim, if you aren't always going about saying you're very good, people end by believing you're very bad. That was what happened to me with Constantia.

The Two Mr. Wetherbys

JAMES [*crosses to table, and leans against chair*]. You deceived her then.

DICK. No, Constantia deceived herself. [*Airily.*] I took no interest at all in the matter.

JAMES [*scornfully*]. Well, the result was a pretty abject fiasco.

DICK. Fiasco! Why it was a triumph! Constantia sulked for six months and then announced her intention of leaving me. For once my perfect candour deserted me. I feigned distress. But it would scarcely have been decent to do otherwise, eh?

[JAMES *makes inarticulate murmur of reprobation.*]

So one auspicious day the lawyers were called in, an amicable separation was arranged, the parties to meet once a year. And that's what brought me here to-day.

JAMES [*indignantly*]. I think it's perfectly shameful.

DICK [*laughing*]. Oh, come, look after the beam in your own eye, old man, and leave me my little mote.

JAMES [*disgusted*]. Don't joke about it. You're always joking.

DICK. That's why I keep so jolly well.
[*Rises, pushes* JAMES.

[JAMES *begins to laugh, finally bursts into a roar.*]

That's right, laugh away, old man, and thank Heaven this deadly lively place hasn't robbed you of the faculty.

[*From this point to end of scene* JAMES *grows*

increasingly cheerful and his gloom quite disappears.
He goes over to fireplace.

JAMES [*sits in arm-chair*].   But don't you feel any remorse ?   Think of Constantia.   You've ruined her life.

DICK.   Not a bit of it.   I know Constantia.   She's as happy as possible.   She doesn't know it, but she is.   She's a good woman and she's got a grievance. What more can she want ?

JAMES.   Still you made her life miserable while you *were* together.

DICK.   Well, she made *my* life miserable too— at least she did her best.   We're quits.

JAMES.   Quits !   Ha, ha !   I remember that's what I said to Maggie.   Do you know, Dick, I hoped you two might patch things up this afternoon and live together again.

DICK.   No, thank you.   I've no ill feeling towards Con.   I even like her in a way.   But I'm not going to live with her.   Con is one of those characters who are much more admirable when you aren't married to them.

[*Crosses back to arm-chair above fireplace and sits.*
JAMES.   You're quite happy as you are ?

DICK.   Quite !   I sleep well, eat well—you don't, Jim—I make no pretence of being better than I am. Rather the contrary.   And I find the world a very pleasant, amusing place.

JAMES.   I wonder how you two ever came to marry ?

DICK [*shrugging shoulders*].   Lunacy, I suppose ! We haven't a taste in common.   Constantia has no

sense of humour. *She* likes solemn asses like Robert.
I don't. By the way, I suppose *you* see a good deal
of Robert ?

[JAMES *nods, laughing.*]

I thought so. And Aunt Clara ?

JAMES. She lives with us.

DICK. Poor chap ! Now, Jim, can you seriously
imagine *my* having Aunt Clara to live with *me ?*
And Robert dropping in every day ?

JAMES. I don't think I can.

DICK. Why don't you turn them out ?

JAMES. My character !

DICK. Oh, it's *that* again, is it ?

JAMES. I'm supposed to be so awfully kind and
considerate and all that. That's the worst of it. If
I were only a brute like you !

DICK [*triumphantly*]. *Now* you begin to see the
point of having *no* character. Try it, old man.
Try it in your bath, as the advertisements say.

JAMES [*ruefully*]. I can't. I've Margaret to
think of.

DICK. She'd get over it—if she's really fond
of you.

JAMES. I daren't face the risk.

DICK. You'd better.

JAMES [*peevishly*]. I *can't*, I tell you. No, I've
got to go on in the old way with Aunt Clara
permanently on the premises, Robert dropping
in to collect subscriptions and Constantia living
next door but one. And I've a reputation for
amiability.

DICK. Poor old chap !

JAMES. 'Tisn't a pretty picture, is it ?

DICK [*jumping up*]. Look here, Jim, you want rousing. You're simply perishing of dulness. Hang billiards! Let's run up to town for an hour, go to the Empire and amuse ourselves. We can be back by twelve!

[JAMES *shakes his head.*]

Half-past eleven then. Come along. [*Pulls him up out of chair.*] Why shouldn't we? It'll do you a world of good.

JAMES [*wavering*]. If Margaret heard of it——

DICK. She won't. After all, 'tisn't the first little jaunt you've had with me, without anybody being the wiser. You'll come?

[*Pulls him out of chair by his arm.*

JAMES [*rising half unwillingly*]. I'm sure I oughtn't——

DICK. Bosh, old man! Come along. I'll look after you. How do the trains go from this confounded place?

JAMES. Pretty often. [*Looks at watch.*] We shall catch one now if we hurry.

DICK [*dashing out for hats and coats and returning immediately*]. Here, get into this. [*Flings him overcoat.*] Hurry up. [*Puts on his own.*]

JAMES. Well, just for an hour. I think I do need shaking up. I feel regularly depressed and out of sorts.

DICK [*dashing to table and pocketing his cigarcase*]. Boredom, my dear fellow. Strong men have died of it!

[*Takes his arm and hurries him out as Curtain falls.*

ACT II   73

The Two Mr. Wetherbys

The Curtain descends for a moment. When it rises again the stage is dark. The scene is the same. Time, three hours later. The sound of a latch-key is heard in front door. Then footsteps in hall. Then dining-room door opens letting in shaft of light from hall. Enter MARGARET *and* ROBERT. MARGARET *turns up electric light, showing dining-room with cloth cleared and biscuits, syphon and glasses on table and whisky decanter on sideboard.*

MARGARET. They're not back yet. At least, I don't see Jim's hat and coat.

ROBERT. Where have they gone ?

MARGARET. To the club, to play billiards.

ROBERT [*gloomily*]. They'll be late then.
[*Puts hat and stick on table.*

MARGARET. I think not.

ROBERT. You don't know Richard !
[*Crosses to fireplace.*

MARGARET [*comes down* L.] Jim will bring him back in good time.

ROBERT. I wonder if it was wise leaving them together ? The influence of a thoroughly depraved nature like Richard's is very insidious.

MARGARET. Oh, with Jim's high character——

ROBERT. Of course. Still there's always a risk.

MARGARET [*with conviction*]. Not with Jim.
[*Sits at table.*

ROBERT [*goes to table and takes three or four biscuits, which he eats till end of scene by fireplace*]. It was curious that I did not see James at the Otaheite meeting last night.

MARGARET. It's so easy to miss people.

ROBERT. Yes. Still there weren't many there. [*Pause.*] Did you see Constantia after her interview to-day?

MARGARET. No.

ROBERT. Then there has not been a reconciliation?

MARGARET. I have heard of none.

ROBERT. I am glad of that. From what she said this afternoon I was afraid Constantia was inclined to forget the past and return to Richard. It must have been a mere momentary weakness.

MARGARET. You don't think we should desire a reconciliation?

ROBERT. My dear Margaret, how *could* we? With *our* principles! Richard is a libertine. That Constantia should so far forget her duty to morality as to forgive him would be deplorable. Think of the example to other men. If a man who treats his wife as Richard did is not to be punished, there would be an end of married happiness altogether.

MARGARET. They have been parted for a year. Is not that sufficient punishment?

ROBERT [*severely*]. Not in my opinion. However deep Richard's repentance, it is too soon to forgive him.

MARGARET. James thinks otherwise.

ROBERT [*sternly*]. James is too good-natured. Too good-natured altogether. He is almost lax—yes, lax is the word—he is not severe enough with his brother. Aunt Clara thinks so too. After the separation he should have set his face against all further relations with him.

MARGARET. But they're in business together.

ROBERT. Except business relations, of course. But to ask him down to stay under his roof! It was weak, Margaret—I am not sure it was not wicked. [*Virtuously.*] Certainly, it is not a thing *I* shall ever do.

MARGARET. I suppose not. Indeed I hardly think Richard would come.

ROBERT. He knows my *principles* too well.

[*Sound of key in front door is heard again. Door slams. Then voices.*

MARGARET. There they are. [*Rises.*

ROBERT [*crossing to table and taking up hat and stick*]. Then I think I'll be going. I do not wish to see more of Richard than I can help. One must not touch pitch!

MARGARET [*going up to door and opening it*]. Is that you, Jim?

JAMES *enters with* DICK—*both have hats and coats.*

JAMES [*entering*]. Yes, dear. [*Kisses her.*] Hullo, Robert, just off?

ROBERT. Yes. It's rather late. Good night.
[*Exit.*

DICK. Now I call that very considerate of Robert.
[*Crosses to fireplace, putting coat on table.*

MARGARET [*coming down towards* JAMES]. Enjoyed your billiards, dear?

JAMES. Thanks, yes, very much.
[*Throws his overcoat on to* DICK's *on table.*

MARGARET. Who was at the Club ?   Any one I know ?

JAMES [*turning away to sideboard*]. No, I think not.   It was rather empty—in fact we saw no one.

MARGARET. How strange !   I wonder why that was ?

JAMES [*diving into sideboard for whisky—slightly confused*]. Of course we were only in the *billiard*-room.   There may have been lots of people in the other rooms.   Drink, Dick ?

[*Puts spirits on table.*]

MARGARET. I see.   Are you going to sit up, dear ?

JAMES. For a little while.   Why ?

MARGARET. Hadn't you better change your coat ?

JAMES. Oh, bother !   I can't go all the way up-stairs.   [*Gives* DICK *his drink.*]

MARGARET. Give it me, dear.   I'm going now, and I'll bring you down an old jacket.

[*He half protests.*]

Oh yes, I will.   It's no trouble.

[*Helps him off with dress coat.*]

JAMES. Angel !   [*Kisses her.*
MARGARET. Goose !

[*Exit* MARGARET.   JAMES *strolls over to fire.*]

DICK [*by table, watching* JAMES, *taking out cigar and cutting off end*]. You're certainly a fluent liar, Jim.

JAMES. Yes. [*Ruefully.*] I've lots of practice, you see.

DICK. *Your* system, eh? I prefer mine. It's not such a tax on the inventive faculties.

JAMES [*half bitterly*]. Just you wait till you're as fond of any one as I am of Margaret, and you'll find yourself lying with the best of them.

DICK. Pessimist!

MARGARET *enters with old jacket,* JAMES *goes up to meet her, while* DICK *stands by fireplace.*

MARGARET. Here you are, dear. [*Helps him into it.*] Don't be late.

JAMES [*kisses her*]. Of course not. Good night.

MARGARET. Good night. [*Kisses him.*] Good night, Richard. [*Exit with little nod.*

DICK [*walks down*] I'm afraid dear Margaret hasn't as warm a regard for me as I deserve.

JAMES [*coming to fireplace*]. I should have thought she managed that!

DICK [*turning*]. Bravo! You're quite epigrammatic to-night. Wonderful what a difference an evening's escape from domesticity makes.

JAMES. Sour grapes, my boy. *You* weren't happy at home, so you want to pretend no one else is.

DICK [*crosses, sits down at table*]. Oh, come, don't pretend you haven't enjoyed yourself to-night. When Kitty Harding was singing " Keep your feet off the grass, dearest," you laughed till I thought you'd have a fit.

JAMES [*giggling at the recollection*]. What a clever little beast she is!

The Two Mr. Wetherbys

DICK. And that fellow who danced! What was the beggar's name?

JAMES [*pause while thinking*]. I forget. I've got the programme in my coat. [*Goes to overcoat on table and feels in pockets.*] Where the deuce is it? [[*An awful pause, during which a look of terror comes into his face.*] Good heavens! I believe it's in the pocket of my dress coat.

[*Searches frantically.*

DICK [*placidly*]. It doesn't matter. We'll look in the morning.

JAMES. But my wife's got it.

[*Throws coat into arm-chair.*

DICK. So she has. But she's not likely to ferret in the pockets, I suppose.

JAMES. Yes, she *will*. She always folds my things if they're lying about, and *takes everything out of the pockets.*

DICK [*jumping up and coming to him.* What a way to treat a wife! Run upstairs at once. You may get there before she's found it.

JAMES [*pale with terror*]. But what can I *do?* She'd want to know what I came up for.

DICK. Say you've left your handkerchief in the pocket—invent something as you go upstairs. You're a better liar than I am. Off with you!

[*Pushes him across and goes to fireplace.*

JAMES. I *daren't!* Suppose she's found it already!

DICK. My dear chap, she will if you don't go at once. Pull yourself together.

JAMES *goes to door, opens it and goes out, returning immediately and coming to arm-chair.*

JAMES [*in a hollow whisper*]. Too late. She's coming downstairs. What on earth's to be done ?

DICK. Steady, Jim. She may not have found it.

JAMES. If she has !

DICK [*calmly*]. Then I should make a clean breast of it if I were you.

JAMES. About to-night ?

DICK. It would be a trifle late to do that !

JAMES [*ruefully*]. I suppose it would.

DICK. Tell her about everything. Save a lot of trouble in the end. And it'll make things easier for you in the future.

JAMES. I dare say you're right. But I simply haven't the pluck.

DICK. Nonsense. Hush, here she is. Shall I make myself scarce ?

JAMES. No. Back me up, for Heaven's sake.

DICK. All right. Courage, old man. [*Leans his back against mantelpiece and surveys scene.*

Door opens, enter MARGARET—*there is a long silence. She stands near the door.*

DICK [*aside to* JAMES]. Better say something.

JAMES [*in a quavering voice*]. Do you want anything, dear ?

[*She is still silent, looking at him steadily.*]

What is it, Maggie ?

MARGARET [*programme in hand—sternly*]. Where were you to-night, James, while Robert and I were out ?

JAMES. Why do you ask such a question ?

MARGARET. Is it such a strange question for a wife to ask ?

JAMES. I went up to London with Dick.

MARGARET. Where ?

JAMES. To the Empire.

[*There is an awkward pause.*]

[*Aside to* DICK.] Own up, can't you ?

DICK [*in his calm tone*]. It was my suggestion, Margaret. I'm the culprit.

MARGARET [*to* JAMES]. Why did you go ?

[*He is silent.*]

DICK. Fact is, I thought he needed livening up. A surfeit of missionary meetings——

MARGARET [*icily*]. I was speaking to my husband. [*Turning again to* JAMES.] Why did you tell me you went to the Club ?

JAMES. We *did mean* to go there.

MARGARET. But you didn't go ? You've not been there at all ?

JAMES. No.

[MARGARET *makes gesture of repulsion and walks down the room.*]

DICK. My dear Margaret, don't fret about *us !* The Empire's a very moral place, far more respectable than most clubs.

MARGARET. I hardly consider *you* a judge of morality, Richard. [*To* JAMES.] Why did you tell me what was not true ?

JAMES. I don't know—I suppose because it would have displeased you.

MARGARET [*bitterly*]. You were very considerate !

JAMES [*stung by her tone—coming down towards her*]. Look here, Maggie, there's no use making a fuss about it. It was just a piece of folly, that's all.

MARGARET. Folly ! To tell your wife a falsehood !

JAMES [*crossly*]. Oh well, there's nothing so startlingly original about *that*.

MARGARET. I didn't expect to hear a speech of that kind from *you*, James ! With *your* high character——

JAMES. Confound my character !

MARGARET [*astonished*]. An evening in Richard's company seems to have produced its effect. Or is that remark the result of your entertainment at a music hall ?

[JAMES *is silent.*]

DICK [*airily*]. Oh, *I*'m the guilty party. The entertainment was irreproachable.

MARGARET. If you would kindly not interrupt, Richard.

[DICK *shrugs his shoulders.*]

Well, James, have you anything to say to me ?

JAMES. Only that I'm sorry, Maggie. I am really.

MARGARET. Is *that* all ?

JAMES [*goaded*]. What do you want me to say ? I can't do more than apologise, can I ? The thing's done now.   Come, Maggie, shake hands and say you forgive me.

> [*Goes towards her holding out hand.*

MARGARET [*refusing his hand*]. No, James, I shall *not* forgive you.

> [JAMES *falls back.*]

You have deceived me deliberately.

DICK [*shocked*]. No, no !

MARGARET. Yes, deliberately.   You are not what I thought you, and I will *never* forgive you.

> [*Turns to go, walking to door.*

JAMES [*alarmed*]. Maggie !

MARGARET [*coldly, turning at door*]. Have you anything more to say ?

DICK [*at* JAMES' *side, quietly*]. Now's your time. Make a clean breast of it.   You'll be glad of it afterwards.

JAMES [*pulling himself together—speaking sharply*]. Stop, Margaret !

> [*She turns again.*]

I *have* something more to say.

> [*She comes towards him again.*]

DICK [*softly—aside*]. Bravo, Jim !

JAMES.   Maggie, I've been wanting to tell you this for a long time——   [*Hesitates.*

MARGARET. Go on.

During this scene MARGARET *gets colder and more angry ;* JAMES *gets more self-possessed.*

JAMES. Maggie, I'm—[*hesitates*]—I'm not what you think me—I'm different—very different.

[*Stops.*

MARGARET. What do you mean ?

JAMES. You think I'm an awfully good sort of chap, who doesn't care about amusement like other men. You think I'm only happy when I'm attending missionary meetings and reading to Aunt Clara. You're mistaken.

MARGARET [*sternly*]. So you weren't at the Otaheite meeting !

JAMES. No, nor the Tobago Diocesan Conference last week, nor the Hairy Ainos Protection Society, nor the Nova Zembla Mission, nor any of them. I don't like missions, they bore me.

MARGARET [*horrified*]. James !

JAMES. Oh yes, they do. You don't know it, but they do. I've gone on pretending for months that I liked them—and other things—just to please you. I've read Aunt Clara her newspaper and given Robert his subscriptions and generally made my life a burden because you liked it. I've done it long enough. I'm going to turn over a new leaf.

MARGARET [*icily*]. And all the time that you were pretending to go to these meetings you were " amusing " yourself at low music-halls, I suppose.

DICK. Not *low* music-halls.

MARGARET. Bah ! How you have fooled me !

JAMES [*complacently*]. Yes, I'm afraid I've not been quite straightforward. But I'm going to reform from to-night.

MARGARET. How long has this been going on?

JAMES. I don't know. A year—eighteen months.

MARGARET [*bitterly*]. And we have only been married two years.

JAMES [*almost genially*]. It was partly your fault, you know. You *would* put me on a sort of pedestal. Of course I tumbled off. You ought to have expected it. You see your standard was too high for me. I tried to live up to it at first, honestly, I did, but it wasn't a success; I wasn't strong enough. But I think *you* ought to share the blame.

MARGARET. Men always throw the blame on women.

JAMES. Only when they deserve it, Maggie. So you see, there's nothing to be angry about. It's just a case of faults on both sides. Shake hands, dear, and give me a kiss.

[*Advances towards her.*

MARGARET [*draws back a pace or two and puts her hands behind her back*]. No, James, I will *not* shake hands. You have fooled and cheated me. Our whole married life has been a sham.

JAMES. No, no, Maggie.

MARGARET [*fiercely*]. Yes, a cheat and a sham! [*Stamps her foot.*] Oh, how I despise you! How I despise myself for having been deceived by you! Did you ever love me at all, I wonder?

[*Half crying—turns away.*

JAMES. You know I did, dear.

MARGARET [*turning, angrily*]. I know nothing.

You deceived me in everything else. Why not in that ?

JAMES. Never mind, Maggie. Make it up and we'll start afresh to-morrow. Forget about all this ; it's past, and I swear I'll always be open with you for the future. I will, really.

MARGARET. The future ! [*Coldly.*] You don't suppose I can *live* with you again after this.

[DICK *raises eyebrows.*]

I should despise myself if I even thought of such a thing.

JAMES [*horrified*]. Maggie !

MARGARET. No, James, I shall leave this house to-morrow. I am no longer your wife.

JAMES [*alarmed*]. You can't. You have no right.

MARGARET. Not legally, perhaps. Morally I should do wrong to remain with you.

JAMES. I shall not allow you to go.

MARGARET. How will you prevent me ? Constantia left Richard for less.

JAMES [*growing more alarmed*]. Maggie, think ! You're angry with me now. It is natural that you should be. But don't punish me too much. Don't leave me. Give me another chance.

MARGARET. And be deceived again ? *No, James !* Indeed I don't think it would be right to forgive you. Men who behave as you have done deserve to suffer.

JAMES [*sadly*]. I didn't expect you would cast me off so readily, Maggie.

MARGARET. You are unjust. You know how I

hate to do it. But I *must*. [*Almost breaking down.*] Oh, Jim, Jim, *why* did you tell me all this? Why didn't you leave me in ignorance?

JAMES [*gently*]. You found me out, dear.

MARGARET. Only about to-night. I could have forgiven you to-night. It's all these months of deception that I *can't* forget.

JAMES. You will.

MARGARET [*bursting into tears*]. No. If it was only to-night it would be different, but now that I know your whole life has been a lie, I cannot live with you any longer. [*With a gulp.*] Good-bye, James. [*Solemnly she walks up towards the door.*

JAMES [*startled*]. Where are you going?

MARGARET [*through her tears*]. To b-b-bed. I shall leave this house to-morrow after breakfast.

[*Exit in a burst of emotion.*

[*There is a pause, during which* DICK *looks half-humorously at* JAMES, *who goes half-way up to door as if to follow, and then turns away. He looks un-utterably depressed.*]

DICK. Curious how much alike sisters are.

JAMES [*brusquely*]. What do you mean?

DICK. I remember an almost similar scene a year ago with Constantia. The marriage tie seems to sit loosely on our family.

JAMES [*snappishly*]. I shall be glad if you won't jest about it.

DICK [*seriously*]. Steady, old man. Don't quarrel with your brother as well as your wife in one evening.

JAMES [*becoming penitent*]. I beg your pardon.

I'm knocked out of time by all this. [*Angrily*]. But I won't have you sneering at Margaret. She's a saint.

DICK. My dear Jim, to say that a lady resembles one's wife isn't usually described as sneering.

JAMES [*impatiently*]. Oh, you know what I mean.

DICK [*putting his hand on* JAMES's *shoulder*]. Poor old boy, you *do* take it bad !

[JAMES *puts his head on his hands and his shoulders heave with sobs.*]

I say, don't do that, for Heaven's sake ! Easy, Jim, easy. She won't go, you know.

JAMES [*turning away*]. She will, I'm sure she will. You don't know Margaret.

DICK. And if she does, there are worse things than being a bachelor again !

JAMES [*laughing in spite of himself*]. That's right—make a joke about it.

DICK. My remark was perfectly serious.

[*Goes to table.*

JAMES [*turning again and coming towards table*]. And the deuce of it all is if I hadn't taken *your* advice and blurted out the whole story like a fool, she would have forgiven me.

DICK [*grimly*]. So she *said.*

[*Pours himself out another drink.*

JAMES. And she would too. [*Crossly.*] I'll trouble you not to question it.

[DICK *shrugs his shoulders.*]

ACT II

This comes of your cursed policy of candour. After this I'll never speak the truth again as long as I live. Never !

[*Soda fizzes loudly into whisky as the curtain falls.*]

QUICK CURTAIN

ACT III

SCENE.—*The drawing-room at the* JAMES WETHERBYS'. *The French windows on to garden are open. The sun shines brilliantly.*

Enter JAMES *and* DICK, *the former looking wretchedly depressed. He goes to fire shivering, and warms hands.*

DICK [*strolling up to open window and looking out*]. Jove, what a glorious morning !

JAMES. Is it ?   I hadn't noticed.

DICK. You didn't eat any breakfast. How the deuce is a fellow to notice anything on an empty stomach ?

JAMES. I wasn't hungry.

DICK. Ah ! *I* was. [*Turning to him and noticing his depression. Then going to him more sympathetically*.] Fretting, Jim ?

JAMES. I suppose so.

DICK [*affectionately*]. What a soft-hearted beggar it is.   Cheer up.

JAMES (*savagely*).   One would think being about to be separated from one's wife was an everyday occurrence to hear you talk !

DICK [*humouring him*]. No, no, not quite that. But will she go ?   That's the question.

JAMES.   You heard what she said last night.

DICK [*easily*]. Oh, I don't attach much importance to *that!*

JAMES [*bitterly*]. I'm afraid I can't share your
confidence.

DICK. Not seen her to-day ?

JAMES. No. She wasn't at breakfast, as you
saw.

DICK [*horrified*]. Has *she* had no breakfast
either ?

JAMES. I don't know.

DICK [*holding up his hands*]. What a household!
Aunt Clara, too ? *She* wasn't down. I assume she
also is fasting ?

JAMES. She always has breakfast in her room.

DICK [*cheerfully*]. I congratulate you. *Robert*
I suppose you're never safe from ?

SERVANT [*announcing*]. Mr. Robert Carne !

DICK [*sitting in arm-chair—sardonically*]. Ah, I
thought so !

Enter ROBERT.

JAMES [*sulkily*]. Good morning.

ROBERT. Good morning, James. I thought I
should find Margaret here.

JAMES. She's not come down yet.

ROBERT. Ah ! I'll wait. [*Sits on ottoman.*

JAMES. She won't be down for some time.
Perhaps you'd better come in later.

ROBERT. I've nothing special to do.

[JAMES *makes gesture of despair at* ROBERT'S *obtuse-
ness behind* ROBERT'S *back. There is a pause. Then
he turns back to* ROBERT *and speaks, hesitating*

between each lie and obviously taxing his powers of invention.]

JAMES. She may not be here for an hour. She has a headache. I advise you to go out for a stroll. She may be a long time yet.

ROBERT. Well, perhaps I'd better come back.

[*Exit.*

[JAMES *gives a sigh of relief.*]

DICK [*looking at* JAMES *curiously*]. My dear Jim, do you *never* speak the truth ?

JAMES. Eh ? No. [*Bitterly*] I suppose I've got out of the habit. [*Sits down.*

DICK [*rises and comes to him*]. Why didn't you kick the beggar out instead of inventing all that rot about Margaret ?

JAMES. I ought to have done so, I suppose. It would have been more straightforward. But I'm hopelessly demoralised. I can't bear hurting the feelings of any one, even an ass like Robert.

DICK. What a good chap you are !

JAMES [*with a bitter laugh*]. Good !

Enter MARGARET. *She looks pale as if after a sleep-less night, but there is no sign of softening in her face.*

[*Rising and going towards her with outstretched hands.*] Good morning, Maggie.

MARGARET. Is that you, James ? I thought you would have gone up to business by now.

[*Ignores hand.*

The Two Mr. Wetherbys

JAMES [*drops hand to his side and turns away*]. I'm not going. I telegraphed up this morning. They'll let me know if there's anything important.

MARGARET. I came to collect a few things out of this room, which I should like to take with me.

JAMES [*hopelessly*]. You are still resolved to go ?

MARGARET. Quite, James.

JAMES. Where ?

MARGARET. To Constantia in the first instance. I dare say she can find room for me for a time. Afterwards, some arrangement will have to be made between us, I suppose. But the lawyers can see to all that. They did in Constantia's case, did they not ?

[*She looks towards* DICK *as she says this, but does not address him directly.*]

DICK (*cheerily*). Oh yes. *They'll* manage it all right. In an amicable separation of this kind, they're invaluable. You leave it to *them*.

[*At back.*

JAMES [*goes towards* MARGARET, *standing a little away from her—in a low voice*]. Is it quite useless to urge you to pause before you do this, Maggie ?

MARGARET. Quite useless, James. My mind is made up. [*Moves away.*] Constantia will be here in a few minutes. I have written to her. Perhaps it would be better if you were not here when she arrived—either of you—it would be painful to everybody.

[*Including* DICK *in her look, but still not addressing him.*]

DICK. Quite right. Let's go out into the garden, Jim, and give Constantia a fair field.

[*Goes towards window, where he stands looking grimly towards the others.*]

JAMES. I shall see you before you go?

MARGARET. If you wish it.

JAMES (*breaking out—crossing to her*). Maggie, if you only knew how sorry I am! How ashamed!

MARGARET (*raising her hand*). Please! If you wish to see me to say good-bye, I am willing, but don't try to change my resolution. You will not succeed.

[*Exeunt* JAMES *and* DICK.]

[MARGARET, *left alone, takes small tray from piano, and wanders round room collecting various trifles, a small clock in case, a couple of books, and a silver scent bottle. She pauses by photograph of* JAMES *on mantelpiece, takes it up, looks at it for some time, half puts it down again, then seems to make up her mind and takes it, adding it to pile on small table.*]

SERVANT [*announcing*]. Mrs. Richard Wetherby.

[*Enter* CONSTANTIA. *Exit* MAID.]

CONSTANTIA (*fussily—going over to her*). My *dear* Margaret, what has happened? I came *at once*. Are you in trouble of any kind? Your note explained nothing.

MARGARET. I thought I would rather tell you myself. I have discovered that James has been deceiving me, and I am leaving him. Can you take me in for a few days?

CONSTANTIA [*astonished*]. Of course, dear, with pleasure—that is, I mean, are you really obliged to take this step ?

MARGARET. I *am* obliged to do so. No other course is open to me.

CONSTANTIA. But, my dear, this is very sudden. James, too ! So high principled as he always appeared ! Are you sure there has been no mistake ?

MARGARET. He has admitted everything.

CONSTANTIA. How extraordinary ! I never should have thought that of James ! But there— you never know *men !* [*Sits down.*] When do you think of coming to me ?

MARGARET. To-day, if you can have me. I am merely putting a few things together to take with me.

[*Adding something to the pile on small table.*]

CONSTANTIA. Quite right, dear. You can't be too careful about *that*. I left such a *lot* of things behind me, when I left Richard, that I wanted afterwards ! Plate, for instance, and knives ! I took not a single spoon or fork, and the same with table linen.

MARGARET (*crosses and sits down*]. I was not thinking of those things. I shall only take a few personal belongings, nothing of value.

CONSTANTIA. Is that *wise*, dear ? Of course James must make you a suitable allowance. My own from Richard was *most* meagre ! And even a small establishment costs so much to start. The merest necessaries are so expensive. And they wear out in no time nowadays.

MARGARET (*listlessly*). I dare say.

CONSTANTIA. But tell me, dear, when did you find out this about James?

MARGARET. Last night. It seems that for months he and Richard have been spending most of their evenings in low dissipation.

CONSTANTIA. Richard was the tempter, of course?

MARGARET [*listlessly*]. I suppose so.

CONSTANTIA [*rising energetically*]. Margaret, there must be an end of this. Richard must not be allowed to exercise his malign influence unfettered. My mind is made up. I shall put a stop to it!

MARGARET. How will you do that?

CONSTANTIA [*Very decidedly*]. By returning to his roof! As long as he is living as a bachelor there is no check on his depravities. But when *I* am with him I can at least see that he keeps within bounds.

MARGARET. You will go back to him? You will forgive him?

CONSTANTIA. No. I shall not forgive him. He has not deserved that. But I shall go back to him. I cannot allow him to retain his liberty any longer. When I separated from him it was to punish his misconduct and give him an opportunity for repentance, not to enable him to plunge deeper into vice and folly. [*Crosses to fire.*

MARGARET. But Constantia! *Ought* you to do this? Won't you be very unhappy? [*Rises.*

CONSTANTIA [*calmly*]. I shall be able to bear it. Indeed, I have not found my life apart from Richard so happy either. The house is very small and the dining-room chimney smokes. [*Sits at desk.*] Of course these things do not *weigh* with me, but they exist. And you must remember that it was *duty* which made me leave my husband, not pleasure. The lot of a woman living apart from her husband has great inconveniences. It may be right that she should do it, it may be *right* that *you* should, dear, but it is not *pleasant!*

MARGARET [*sits on ottoman—bitterly*]. The life of a woman who lives with a husband she no longer loves is not pleasant either.

CONSTANTIA. No doubt. [*In a practical tone.*] Still, of the two, I think I prefer it. [*Pause.*] And in any case we can only take the course which we believe to be *right*. *My* duty is clearly to return to Richard and to watch over him more carefully in future.

MARGARET. Then you will not be able to take me in for a few days?

CONSTANTIA. No, dear. I shall be going back to town with Richard this afternoon. But you can have my house for the present with pleasure. Houses are always better occupied, aren't they? And I shall probably not be able to let it immediately.

MARGARET. You intend to speak to Richard to-day?

CONSTANTIA [*briskly*]. Yes. At once, if you will kindly send for him.

MARGARET [*rises*]. Very well. [*Rings bell.*] And now if you don't mind I'll go upstairs and finish my packing.

Enter MAID.

The Two Mr. Wetherbys

Will you ask Mr. Richard to come here, Jane? He is in the garden. Take these things upstairs when you have done so.

> [*Points to things on sofa and exit.*

> [*Exit* MAID, *returning a moment later with* DICK. *Then exit* MAID *with tray full of things.*]

DICK. Hullo, Constantia! You here? You want to see me?¦

CONSTANTIA. Yes, Richard.

DICK. But this isn't in the agreement. The agreement said that we were to meet once a year. I really can't talk to you two days running!

CONSTANTIA. This is not a time for jesting.

DICK. It never is—with you, Constantia!

> [*She makes impatient gesture.*]

Well, what do you want to say to me?

CONSTANTIA. Richard, I have heard of your shocking behaviour.

DICK. Not for the first time, I am sure.

CONSTANTIA. It appears, from what Margaret has told me, that you now abuse your liberty as shamelessly as you formerly abused your position as a husband. In the one case you made *my* life wretched. In the other you lead others into temptation.

DICK. Meaning poor old Jim.

CONSTANTIA. I mean your unhappy brother James.

DICK [*nodding*]. I suppose it's the same person.

CONSTANTIA. What I have now to say to you is,

98   ACT III

that I cannot permit you to be a source of moral contamination to others any longer.

DICK. I see. You're going to keep your eye on me from Norwood ? Very sporting of you to warn me beforehand.

CONSTANTIA. No, Richard. I am going to return to you as your wife ! [*Rises.*

DICK [*his jaw drops*]. Oh no, you're not ! [*Moves away.*]

CONSTANTIA. I beg your pardon.

DICK. My dear Constantia, pray dismiss this idea from your mind altogether. You will not return to me because I decline to receive you.

CONSTANTIA [*astonished*]. You refuse ?

DICK. Of course I refuse. You don't love me. You told me that yesterday. And now your only idea in returning to me is to keep an eye on my moral character. You don't suppose I shall *like* that, do you ?

CONSTANTIA [*frigidly*]. It was not intended that you should.

DICK. Precisely. So I decline to submit myself to the experiment.

CONSTANTIA. I shall insist upon it. [*Loftily.*] It is the *duty* of a husband and wife to live together.

DICK. It's taken you some time to find out that ! [*Moves away slightly.*

CONSTANTIA [*takes a step after him—after a pause*]. Tell me, Richard, what is your reason for this refusal ? You must have a reason.

DICK. My dear Constantia, it's simple enough, I no longer love you.

CONSTANTIA [*starting back*]. You dare tell me that !

DICK. Why not ? You no longer love *me*. You told me so yesterday.

CONSTANTIA [*walks away*]. There's some other reason. I'm sure of it. If you no longer care for me it must be because you have met some one else.

DICK [*sits*]. My dear, don't be childish.

CONSTANTIA [*turning*]. Oh, you can't put me off in that way. A man doesn't want to live apart from his wife in this discreditable manner unless there is some other woman he loves better.

DICK. What shocking ideas you moral people have.

CONSTANTIA [*coming and standing over him*]. If you were not irreclaimably vicious you would welcome this chance of a reconciliation.

DICK. Vicious ? Nonsense, I'm not vicious. I'm a very moral person.

CONSTANTIA. Then you deceived me grossly. You always *told* me you were vicious.

DICK. I think not.

CONSTANTIA. Well, when I said so, you never denied it.

DICK. I always used to let you have your own way. That's why you left me. Women like to be tyrannised over.

CONSTANTIA [*she takes a few paces and turns—controlling herself with difficulty*]. Will you answer me one question ?

DICK [*blandly*]. No. I don't think I will. In fact this whole interview is most irregular. You must keep it for next year.

CONSTANTIA. You're unbearable.

DICK [*rises, triumphantly*]. That's why we're so much better apart. I'm sure you feel that ?

CONSTANTIA [*coming up to him, fiercely*]. You won't get rid of me so easily.

DICK [*sweetly*]. Not altogether, perhaps. But the relative freedom I at present enjoy suits me well enough.

CONSTANTIA [*furious*]. I'll find a way of punishing you for this !

DICK [*laughing*]. Threats ! My dear Con, you shock me. Why should you object ? You'll be happy enough. You'll have Margaret with you, you know.

[CONSTANTIA *makes a gesture of rage. She walks away from him.*]

As for Jim, he will share my flat in Maddox Street. It's big enough for two.

[JAMES *passes French window.* DICK *calls to him.*]

Won't you, Jim ?

JAMES [*coming to window*]. What did you say ?

DICK. I was telling Constantia you and I were going to settle down together in Maddox Street.

CONSTANTIA (*crosses to* DICK *with gesture of fury*]. Brute ! [*Exit, in a towering passion.*

DICK. Come in, Jim. I never could resist the temptation to chaff Constantia.

JAMES [*coming down, sarcastically*]. I suppose she *liked* that ?

DICK. If she did, she concealed the feeling very

successfully. But how about you, old man? *You* don't look very bright. Wife not forgiven you yet?

JAMES. No. She's determined to leave me.

DICK. Lucky fellow! *My* wife wants to *return* to *me!* I'm far more to be pitied.

JAMES [*irritably*]. I wish to Heaven you'd be serious sometimes.

DICK. Serious? I'm deuced serious. Why, I tell you, my dear chap, if I hadn't been absolutely rude to Constantia, she'd have thrown herself into my arms and we should have had to begin married life all over again! I shouldn't have liked *that* at all.

JAMES. Why did she want to go back? It seems an odd taste.

DICK. Taste had nothing to do with it. It was pure conscientiousness on her part. She thinks she ought to look after me.

JAMES. And you refused to take her back?

DICK [*nods*]. Certainly.

JAMES [*disgusted*]. You must be an absolute brute. [*Sits.*

DICK. Why? She left me of her own choice. I'm not going to be sent about my business and then whistled back again at a moment's notice. What would you say—[*crosses to him*]—if Margaret told you she'd altered her mind and wasn't going to leave you after all?

JAMES [*enthusiastically*]. Say? Why, that she was the dearest, kindest, most forgiving little soul in the world.

DICK [*horrified*]. My dear fellow!

JAMES. Confound you, Dick, can't you understand that I *love* Margaret—that there's nothing on earth I wish so much as to be reconciled to her ?

DICK. And go back to the old slavery ?

JAMES. It wasn't slavery. It was happiness.

[DICK *gasps.*]

DICK. Well, you certainly have the most curious conception of happiness. But there, go back to your Margaret, if you must !

JAMES. If I only could !

DICK. But don't expect me to take back Constantia, because I sha'n't.

JAMES. I don't believe you're serious.

DICK. I'm perfectly serious. [*Looking at him keenly.*] Are you ?

JAMES. About Margaret ? Of course.

[DICK *shrugs his shoulders.*]

Dash it, man, one would think it was *unusual* for a husband to want to be reconciled to his wife !

DICK. 'Tisn't what you'd call *common !* But there, it's your taste. Send her down to me. Say I've something to say to her.

[JAMES *rises.*]

I dare say I can bring her to reason.

[*In an offhand way.*

JAMES. She won't come.

DICK. Oh yes, she will—from curiosity.

[*Exit* JAMES *disgusted at this parting piece of cynicism.*]

[*While he is away* DICK *strolls about room, examining philistine decorations with every sign of contempt. Notices gap on mantelpiece where* JIM'S *picture used to be. Whistles. Enter* MARGARET. *He turns hurriedly and stands with back to fireplace.*]

MARGARET. You wish to speak to me ?

DICK. Yes. Sit down.

MARGARET [*sits on ottoman*]. I should tell you at once that if your intention is to plead on James's behalf, you are only wasting your time.

DICK [*airily*]. Oh, it isn't. I think Jim's rather well out of it.

MARGARET [*with frozen dignity*]. I beg your pardon ?

DICK. It isn't half bad being a bachelor again, at least that's my experience.

MARGARET. James is not of your opinion.

DICK. He will be. Not at first, of course, but afterwards, and anyhow he'll get accustomed to it. It's astonishing how quickly men get *used* to things. He'll drop back into the old bachelor ways. No Aunt Clara ! [*Impressively.*] No Robert ! Oh, *he'll* be happy enough. You needn't fret about *him !*

MARGARET. It's not true. James is not like that.

DICK. My dear Margaret, men are very much alike. He'll get to enjoy his freedom as I have done.

MARGARET [*fiercely*]. He won't ! He won't ! You're heartless and selfish. You don't *feel* at all. Jim loves me.

The Two Mr. Wetherbys

DICK [*pause—quietly*]. I used to love Constantia.

MARGARET. Used to love ?

DICK. Yes. [*With obvious sincerity.*] People say that love never dies. On the contrary love is killed, oh so easily. A word, a look, moments of temper, inopportune tears. How they kill love !

MARGARET. I don't believe you.

DICK. Oh yes, you do. And besides these, there are other things—boredom, relations—you're not very fortunate in the matter of relations, are you ? Little failures of tact and taste, little errors of judgment, all these contain a drop of the poison which may help to kill love !

MARGARET [*wondering*]. Why do you speak to me like this ? You are quite serious. I thought you were never serious.

DICK. I'm not often—fortunately.

MARGARET (*puzzled*). But why now ? [*Rising angrily.*] I see what it is. This is a trap. You want to make me forgive James.

DICK [*in his most exasperating manner*]. My dear Margaret, be sensible. Sit down. Why on earth should *I* want you to forgive Jim ? I *like* him !

MARGARET [*stung*]. What do you mean ?

DICK. You see, if you leave Jim *I* shall see a lot more of him than I do now. As far as I am concerned the more completely you sever your connection with him the better.

MARGARET [*triumphantly*]. But he wouldn't be happy.

DICK. Ah ! we don't agree about that.

The Two Mr. Wetherbys

MARGARET [*sitting down*]. Then why did you send for me ? Why have you spoken to me at all ? If you would rather I left James why need you do anything but just leave us to part as we *were* doing ?

DICK. *Were ?* Your resolution is wavering, you see.   [*Moves slightly towards her.*

MARGARET [*hotly*]. It is *not !*

DICK [*calmly*]. I misunderstand you, then. So much the better for me. *I* get Jim. You don't !

MARGARET [*bewildered*]. I don't understand. You haven't told me yet why you're trying to bring us together—if you are trying.

DICK [*dispassionately*]. It's a sort of random benevolence on my part. I have fits of it.

MARGARET (*peevishly*). What *do* you mean ?

DICK. The fact is, I was talking to poor old Jim a few minutes ago, and he really did seem most awfully fond of you and all that, in spite of the way you've behaved——

MARGARET [*rising angrily*]. *I've* behaved ! Thank you, Richard. That will do. I told you it was useless for you to plead on James's behalf. I am now sure of it.   [*Walks away.*

DICK [*laughing*]. Come back, Margaret. You misunderstand me. If you would kindly have let me finish my sentence.

MARGARET. Well ?
                [*Turns to face him but does not come back.*

DICK. Let me see, where was I ? Oh, I found that Jim was awfully fond of you—absurdly so it seemed to me—and you're awfully fond of him too, you know, though you won't admit it at present.

MARGARET. I don't see that that is any reason why you should have interfered.

DICK [*impatiently*]. My dear Margaret, when I see a woman deliberately throwing away her own happiness, I think it's only kind to warn her. That's all.

MARGARET. *Her* happiness?

DICK. Yes. [*Pause.*] Jim will get over this all right, as I said. Men do. They're tough. And they've lots of distractions. It's different with women. [*Coldly.*] So I thought I'd just give you a hint before it was too late.

MARGARET [*sarcastically*]. Isn't it rather late for *you* to begin to consider *me?*

DICK. I dare say. But it's not too late for you to consider yourself.

MARGARET [*haughtily*]. I haven't the least idea what you mean by that.

DICK. Sit down and I'll try to make myself clear.

[*She sits. He sits beside her on the ottoman.
MARGARET on the right. DICK on the left.*]

MARGARET. Well?

DICK. Do you know what passed between myself and Constantia this morning?

MARGARET. Yes. A reconciliation.

DICK. No. Your sister wished for one. At least she wished to patch up our marriage somehow. I refused.

MARGARET. You refused ?

DICK. Yes. [*Pause.*] I'm happier as I am.

MARGARET. And Constantia ? Didn't you think at all of her ?

DICK. Constantia made her choice a year ago. She can't alter it now.

MARGARET. And are you never going to live with her again ? Never at all ?

DICK [*cheerfully*]. *Never!* On that point I am quite clear. [*There is a pause.*

MARGARET [*slowly*]. I still don't see what all this has to do with *me*.

DICK [*airily*]. Merely a parallel case. That's all.

MARGARET [*in a whisper*]. Parallel ?

DICK [*sternly*]. Yes. I loved Constantia once. Jim loves you now. Constantia sulked with me, badgered me, bored me, finally left me as you are leaving Jim. Poor woman, she thought she would be happy living alone. At least she thought she would be contented. So do you. She was mistaken. You can see it in her face, the lonely look of the woman who has no home. And we have only been separated a year ! Yet she so hates her present life that this morning nothing but my direct refusal to receive her prevented her from returning to me. What a situation ! How humiliating and disastrous ! Think carefullty, Margaret, before you do as she did.

MARGARET [*half to herself*]. What an escape ! What an escape !

DICK. You *will* think carefully ? Not for Jim's sake, Margaret, *but for your own.*

[MARGARET *bursts into tears*.]

[*Rises*.] There, there, that's all right, dry your eyes and then go and make it up with Jim.

MARGARET [*trying to stifle her sobs*]. B— b— but will he forgive me? Will he make it up?

DICK [*grimly*]. Oh yes, he'll forgive you all right.

MARGARET [*rising and drying her eyes*]. It's very unjust. Men always have the best of it. *They* do wrong and *we* suffer.

DICK. Ah well, you manage to make it pretty disagreeable for them too sometimes.

MARGARET [*half crying*]. I thought I was doing right. Jim behaved very badly. It was my *duty* to punish him.

DICK. You don't call punishing your husband *duty*? *I* call it pleasure.

MARGARET [*laughing through her tears*]. You're very horrid! But you meant this kindly. You're not really *bad*, Dick. I see that now.

DICK [*alarmed*]. For Heaven's sake don't begin putting *me* on a pedestal! It wouldn't suit me at all. [*Going to door, opens it and calls*.] Jim! Jim! [*To* MARGARET.] Come, summon up a smile to greet your husband. Ever such a little one!

[*She smiles faintly. She crosses, and turns towards him*.]

Enter JIM.

Jim, go to your wife and tell her you're heartily

ashamed of yourself and will never do anything wrong again, and perhaps she'll forgive you. I'll go upstairs and finish packing. I sha'n't be two minutes. [*Exit hastily.*

JAMES [*coming towards her.*] Margaret! Is it true? Will you forgive me this time?

MARGARET. Yes, Jim, if you'll promise never to hide anything from me again.

[*Embraces him.*

JAMES. Angel! Of course I promise. I'll never hide anything from you in future. And I'll never go anywhere with Dick again as long as I live!

MARGARET. Oh no, Jim, you mustn't say that. I've changed my opinion about Dick. I believe he's quite good really, nearly as good as you are, only not so serious. I should like him to come and stay with us. He's fond of you, Jim.

JAMES. What will Aunt Clara say to that?

MARGARET. Aunt Clara will not be here. She must go away; and Robert too. In future we must have our house to ourselves, and live our lives in our own way.

JAMES [*embracing*]. Margaret, you're a trump! But I'll deserve it. I swear I will. I'll do whatever you wish. [*Draws her down on sofa beside him.*

MARGARET. Dear old Jim.

[*Strokes his hair affectionately.*

Enter DICK *with bag and overcoat.*

DICK. Hullo, not finished yet?

[MARGARET *moves away from him hastily.*]

The Two Mr. Wetherbys

JAMES. Confound you, Dick, don't interrupt.
[*Possesses himself of* MARGARET's *hand.*
DICK. Not for worlds. But as my train goes in ten minutes, I thought you might find time to say good-bye to me. [*Comes towards them.*]
JAMES [*rising*]. You're not going before lunch?
MARGARET. Do stay.
DICK. No. [*Getting into coat.*] The atmosphere of this place is altogether too connubial. I must get back to my lonely flat in Maddox Street, where no wives are admitted. Good-bye, Maggie. Good-bye, Jim. Don't be too *good*, either of you! And when you see Constantia, tell her I've [JAMES *and* MARGARET *cross together*] decided to remain a grass widower permanently.

[*Turns to go, picking up bag and hat.* MARGARET *and* JAMES *stand hand in hand. As he reaches the door, enter* CONSTANTIA *dressed as for a journey. In her hand she carries a dressing-bag.*]

Hullo, Con, I was just speaking of you. What *is* the use of that confounded agreement if you keep popping up in this way? What are *you* doing here?
CONSTANTIA. I came to find *you*, Richard.
DICK. But this is quite out of order. You were to see me once a year, not twice a day. Besides, I'm just off to London.
CONSTANTIA. I also am going to London.
DICK. By this train?
CONSTANTIA. Yes.

DICK [*crosses*]. Very well. You've just time to catch it. [*Sits down*] I'll take the next.

CONSTANTIA. No, Richard, we shall go together.
[*Comes towards him.*

DICK. What !

CONSTANTIA. I have made up my mind to forgive you. I consider it my duty.

DICK [*with the calmness of despair*]. There seems to be a perfect epidemic of forgiveness down here just now. Here's Margaret who has made it up with Jim, and there they stand holding one another's hands in a manner that's perfectly sickening.

[MARGARET *pulls her hand away guiltily.*]

And now *you* want to forgive *me !* I don't want to be forgiven ! I *won't* be forgiven !

CONSTANTIA [*sternly*]. Margaret ! Is this true ?

MARGARET. Yes, Connie.

CONSTANTIA. Indeed ! Well, I only hope you will not live to regret it. You appear to me to have acted with undue precipitation !

JAMES. We're going to risk it !

CONSTANTIA [*with grunt of disapproval, turning to* DICK]. Well, Richard. I am ready.

DICK. I'm not. I decline to allow you to come with me.

CONSTANTIA [*firmly*]. Nothing but physical violence will prevent me.

DICK [*rises, reproachfully*]. Look here, Con, is this fair ? I allowed you to leave me when you wanted to. *You've* no right to change your mind now. It's fickle, that's what I call it. Beastly fickle !

CONSTANTIA. This is not a moment for jesting.

DICK [*disgusted*]. It certainly isn't !

CONSTANTIA [*sternly*]. Then if you will take up your bag, perhaps we had better start.

DICK. I'm dashed if I will. I can't take you to Maddox Street. You'd be awfully uncomfortable there.

CONSTANTIA. I shall do very well. You said there was room for two only this morning.

[DICK *makes a gesture of despair.*]

MARGARET [*coaxingly*]. Dick, be *nice* to her. You're not hard-hearted really, though you like to pretend to be. Take her back.

DICK. Look here, Maggie, I call that pretty rough. Is this my reward for reconciling you to your husband ?

MARGARET. Well, I'm only trying to reconcile you to your wife.

DICK [*disgusted*]. Dash it all ! Don't joke about it. *One* humorist is enough in any family.

JAMES. Make it up, old man. It isn't half bad being married after all, eh, Maggie ? And you can't prevent her from coming unless you call in the police ! You only separated by mutual consent.

DICK (*resigning himself*). Very well. Look here, Con, if you'll say you're sorry for the way you've treated me, and will let me do everything that I please in future and always laugh at my jokes, I'll forgive you. I can't say fairer than that.

MARGARET. Say yes, Connie.

Dick [*to her more kindly*].   Come, Con, do the thing handsomely.   Is it yes ?

CONSTANTIA.   Yes, Richard.

[*They shake hands.*]

CURTAIN.

[*At second curtain* CONSTANTIA *is by door, followed by* DICK *carrying BOTH the bags.*]

THE END

THE RETURN OF THE PRODIGAL

A COMEDY FOR FATHERS

" Character is Fate "

CHARACTERS

SAMUEL JACKSON.

MRS. JACKSON, *his wife.*

HENRY JACKSON, *their elder son.*

EUSTACE JACKSON, *their younger son.*

VIOLET JACKSON, *their daughter.*

SIR JOHN FARINGFORD, BART.

LADY FARINGFORD, *his wife.*

STELLA FARINGFORD, *their daughter.*

DR. GLAISHER.

THE REV. CYRIL PRATT, *the Rector.*

MRS. PRATT, *his wife.*

BAINES, *Butler at the Jacksons'.*

TWO FOOTMEN.

The action of the play takes place at Chedleigh Court, the Jacksons' house in Gloucestershire, Act. I in the Drawing-room, Act II in the Breakfast-room, Act III on the Lawn, and Act IV in the Drawing-room again. Chedleigh, as everybody knows, is famous for its cloth mills.

THE RETURN OF THE PRODIGAL

ACT I

SCENE. *The* JACKSONS' *drawing-room, a handsome room suggesting opulence rather than taste. Not vulgar but not distinguished. Too full of furniture, pictures, knick-knacks, chair covers, plants in pots. Too full of everything. The door is on the right. On the grand piano, which is on the opposite side of the room from the door, are large bowls of flowers, photograph frames, and other inappropriate things. There are also plants in the fireplace, as it is summer and that is the* JACKSONS' *conception of the proper way to adorn a fireplace and a suitable place for growing plants. Easy chairs everywhere. The room is lighted by electricity, but when the curtain rises only a few of the lights are turned on. The time is after dinner on a summer evening.*

When the curtain rises the stage is empty. Then the door opens and LADY FARINGFORD *enters, followed by her daughter* STELLA, MRS. PRATT, VIOLET JACKSON, *and, after an interval,* MRS. JACKSON.

MRS. JACKSON [*heard calling to her husband before she enters*]. You won't stay too long over your cigars, will you, Samuel ? [*She comes in.*] I always notice the gentlemen stay far too long in the dining-room unless they're specially told not to. Now, Lady Faringford, where will you sit? Try this sofa.

LADY FARINGFORD [*selecting the most comfortable corner of the sofa*]. Thank you.

MRS. JACKSON. That's right. Mrs. Pratt, where shall I put you? No, don't go there. That's such a long way off. Come here. [*Drags up arm-chair near* LADY FARINGFORD *with hospitable inelegance.* MRS. PRATT *sits.*] Are you all right, Stella?

STELLA [*who has already found a seat*]. Quite, thanks, Mrs. Jackson.

VIOLET. Where will you go, mother?

MRS. JACKSON. I'm going to sit here. Wait till I turn on some more light. [*Goes to door and does so.*] That's better!

[MRS. JACKSON *takes seat by* LADY FARINGFORD. VIOLET *sits by* STELLA *and, after a decent interval, draws work-basket towards her and quietly begins to knit.*]

LADY FARINGFORD. I do envy you your electric light, Mrs. Jackson. Lamps are so troublesome. The servants are always setting themselves on fire with them.

MRS. JACKSON [*comfortably*]. It *is* convenient, isn't it?

LADY FARINGFORD. How long have you had it?

MRS. JACKSON. Only about eighteen months. We had it brought here at the same time that they were putting it in at the Mill. It seemed a pity not to as it was so close. And now I don't know what we should do without it.

MRS. PRATT.　I saw it was all on at the Mill as we passed to-night.

MRS. JACKSON.　Yes.　They can work much later now it's been put in.　That was Henry's idea.　It was almost impossible to work overtime profitably before on account of the light.　Now the Mill often works night and day when there's a pressure.

STELLA.　Surely the workmen must sleep sometimes ?

MRS. JACKSON [*placidly*].　They have different sets of workmen, I believe.　But you must ask Henry.　He knows all about it.

LADY FARINGFORD.　Mr. Jackson seems pretty cheerful about his election prospects.

MRS. JACKSON.　Yes.　I do hope he'll get in.　It will be such an amusement for him.

MRS. PRATT.　It would certainly be most regrettable if Mr. Ling were elected.　He is a dissenter. The Rector says a clergyman should have no politics, but I say a clergyman with no politics is never made a bishop.

LADY FARINGFORD.　I trust the Rector will not allow Mr. Ling to use the Parish Room for any of his meetings.

MRS. PRATT.　I'm afraid he will.　He says he can't make distinctions between the two parties.　If he lends the room to one he must lend it to the other.

LADY FARINGFORD.　Then he had better lend it to neither.　That will answer the purpose quite well. For Mr. Jackson can easily hire some place for his meetings while Mr. Ling cannot.　It is such a comfort that all the rich people about here are

Conservatives. But I believe the same thing may be noticed in other parts of the country. It almost seems like a special Providence.

MRS. JACKSON. I hope Sir John thinks my husband will get in ?

LADY FARINGFORD. Oh yes, I think so. It's unfortunate that Mr. Ling is so popular. Only with quite vulgar people no doubt, Nonconformists and so forth. But even then they have votes unfortunately. Still Mr. Jackson employs a large number of people and they will vote for him of course—or what's the use of being an employer ?— and if he is sufficiently liberal with his subscriptions——

MRS. JACKSON. I believe my husband subscribes to *everything*.

LADY FARINGFORD. Then I'm sure he'll get in. It's a pity he won't have the Illingtons' support, by the way. They have a great deal of influence in their part of the county.

MRS. PRATT [*horrified*]. Surely Sir James hasn't turned Radical ?

LADY FARINGFORD. No, no. Not so bad as *that!* But I hear he's quite ruined. His racing stable has cost him a fortune in the last few years, and he's never won a single race. Braden will be to let in the autumn.

MRS. JACKSON. Poor Sir James. He will feel parting with the place dreadfully.

LADY FARINGFORD. It's his own fault. He ought never to have made that absurd marriage. Mary Illington—she was Mary Tremayne, you know, one of the Wiltshire Tremaynes—hadn't a sixpence.

What will become of that boy of theirs at Eton I can't think. They'll never be able to pay his school bills.

MRS. JACKSON. Public schools *are* dreadfully expensive, aren't they ? I remember when Eustace, my second boy, was at Harrow—Henry was never at a Public School—his bills were terribly high.

MRS. PRATT. I wonder whom we shall have at Braden. I do hope they will be Church people. The Scalebys, who took Astley Park, play tennis on Sundays and seem to me to be little better than heathens. It sets such a bad example.

LADY FARINGFORD. The county is changing sadly. Half the old houses have changed hands, and the new people are usually quite dreadful. If this sort of thing goes on there won't be a single person fit to speak to within twenty miles.

[*Silence falls upon the company as* LADY FARING-FORD *makes this tactful remark, but that lady seems quite unconscious of the effect she has produced. Then* STELLA *breaks the awkward pause.*]

STELLA [*to* VIOLET]. What are you working at ?

VIOLET. A pair of socks for Old Allen. I always give him a pair for his birthday. That's about a month from now.

MRS. PRATT. I hope you and Mrs. Jackson have got a lot of things ready for the Mission Room Fund Bazaar, Violet ? We want to clear off our debt, and, if possible, have something in hand as well.

VIOLET. Oh yes. I've done some things and so has mother. I'll send them up in a day or two.

ACT I   123

MRS. PRATT. And thank *you* so much, Lady Faringford, for the embroidered tea-cloth you sent. It is *sure* to sell!

LADY FARINGFORD. Let us hope so. It's extremely ugly. I bought it at the Kettlewell sale of work last year intending to give it to my poor sister Adelaide. But afterwards I hadn't the heart. So I sent it to your bazaar instead.

[*Another awkward pause. Poor* MRS. PRATT *smiles nervously.*]

MRS. JACKSON. Vi, my dear, won't you play us something?

STELLA. Do, Vi. We never have any music at the Hall now Fraulein Schmidt has gone.

VIOLET. Very well, if you'd really like it.

[*Rises and goes to piano.*

LADY FARINGFORD [*to* MRS. JACKSON]. You remember her? She was Stella's governess. Quite an intelligent, good creature. But I dare say you never met her. She never used to come down to dinner. I always think German governesses so much more satisfactory than English. You see, there's never any question about having to treat *them* as ladies. And then they're always so plain. That's a great advantage. And German is such a useful language, far more useful for a young girl than French. There are so many more books she can be allowed to read in it. French can be learnt later— and should be in my opinion.

MRS. PRATT [*who has recovered from the shock of the tea-cloth incident*]. I quite agree with you, Lady Faringford. But the Rector is less strict in these matters. He allowed my girls to begin French directly they went to school, at Miss Thursby's. But I'm bound to say they never seem to have learnt any. So perhaps it did no harm.

MRS. JACKSON. Yes, I have always heard Miss Thursby's was an excellent school.

[VIOLET *begins to play. The piece selected is the second movement of Beethoven's twenty-seventh Sonata, sometimes called " The Conversation with the Beloved." Before she has played a dozen bars, however,* BAINES, *the* JACKSONS' *butler, enters, and she stops.*]

BAINES [*going up to* MRS. PRATT, *and speaking in an undertone*]. If you please, Madam, Simmonds is here asking if you could see him. They sent him on from the Rectory.

MRS. PRATT. Simmonds ? Did he say his business ?

BAINES [*coughs discreetly*]. Something about *Mrs.* Simmonds, I think, Madam.

MRS. PRATT. Of course, I remember. I will come in a moment. [*Rising.*] You'll excuse me, won't you, dear Mrs. Jackson ? It's Mrs. Simmonds. Foolish woman, she's had another baby. Her husband is in the hall. I shall probably have to run over to the Rectory for some things for her.

MRS. JACKSON [*rising at once*]. Oh no, you mustn't do that. I am sure we have everything necessary here, soup and jelly and flannel, and anything else you think wise. And, of course, they will want some money. I had better come and see Simmonds with you. Then we can tell the housekeeper to put the things together for him.

MRS. PRATT.   But it's giving you so much trouble.

MRS. JACKSON.   Not in the least.   It's no trouble. And I can't have you running away and leaving us before the Rector has finished his cigar.   That would never do.

VIOLET [*rising*].   Can I do anything, mother ?

MRS. JACKSON.   No, dear.   I can manage quite well.   You stay here and entertain Lady Faringford and Stella.   We sha'n't be five minutes.

[MRS. JACKSON *hurries out beaming with benevolence, closely attended by* MRS. PRATT.   BAINES *follows them out with dignity, refusing to allow his composure to be ruffled by so trivial an incident as the arrival of a cottager's baby.*]

VIOLET.   Poor Mrs. Simmonds.   I do hope the baby will be all right.

LADY FARINGFORD.   I have no doubt it will. When people have far more children already than is either convenient or necessary their babies always exhibit extraordinary vitality.   Nothing seems to kill them.   But you were going to play to us, dear.

[VIOLET *returns to piano and begins to play again.* STELLA *listens with obvious pleasure.*   LADY FARINGFORD *fidgets, picks up book, yawns, puts it down again, and generally shows by her manner that she is bored to death by the music.   Presently she succeeds in attracting* STELLA'S *attention by tapping gently with her fan, and beckons to her.*   STELLA *gets up resignedly and goes over to sit by her mother, who begins to talk to her under cover of the music.*]

By the way, Stella, how are things going between you and Henry ?

STELLA. What do you mean, mother?

LADY FARINGFORD. Has he asked you to marry him yet?

STELLA. No.

LADY FARINGFORD. Strange! I thought he would have done so before now. I have given him several opportunities.

STELLA. Mother!

LADY FARINGFORD. He is going to, I suppose?

STELLA. I don't know.

LADY FARINGFORD. Nonsense, child. Of course you do. A girl always knows when a man wants to propose to her, unless she is perfectly idiotic. He will certainly propose if you give him proper encouragement. [*Persuasively.*] And when he does you will accept him?

STELLA [*thoughtfully*]. I'm not sure.

LADY FARINGFORD. Not sure? Why not? You like him, don't you? . . . I can't think who invented music after dinner. One can hardly hear oneself speak. . . . As I was saying, you like him?

STELLA. Oh yes. I like him.

LADY FARINGFORD. Then of course you will accept him. When a man proposes to a girl and she likes him, and he is well off and otherwise eligible, she should always accept him.

STELLA. But—[*hesitates*]—I don't love him, mother.

LADY FARINGFORD. My dear, you must not expect impossibilities. Love matches aren't very common among people of our class. And they're by no means always successful either. Quite the contrary. If you marry a man you like you may come to love him—in time. But if you marry the man you love you may easily come to loathe him.

STELLA [*sighs*]. Well, I suppose I shall have to marry him in the end.

LADY FARINGFORD. Of course you will. And I'm sure you might do a great deal worse. The Jacksons are really very well off. The business has grown enormously in the last few years. Of course, they're *parvenus*. But everybody one meets nowadays is either a *parvenu* or a pauper. And really girls are so numerous just now they can't afford to be as particular as they were. Henry is the only son.

STELLA. No, mother. There's Eustace.

LADY FARINGFORD. I don't count Eustace. He went away years ago—to one of the Colonies, I believe—and doubtless came to a bad end. Probably he's dead by now.

STELLA. Mother! How can you say such terrible things!

LADY FARINGFORD. Nonsense. Of course he's dead. And a very good thing, too. . . . . Really, what a noise our good Violet is making. . . . . If he weren't dead one would have heard something of him. That sort of young man always makes himself felt by his relatives as long as the breath's in his body.

STELLA. But if he's abroad——

LADY FARINGFORD. Then he would write—for money. People in the Colonies always do write for money. You don't remember him, do you?

STELLA. Hardly at all. I've seen him, of course.

LADY FARINGFORD. Ah! He was a handsome

fellow. Clever, too. But a thorough detrimental.
It's just as well he went to the Colonies. No, my
dear, you can't do better than accept Henry. He'll
be quite a rich man some day, and he's really very
fairly presentable. And his father will get into
Parliament. Not that that means anything nowadays. Here he is.

[LADY FARINGFORD *leans back in her corner of the
sofa, and makes a decent pretence of having listened to
the music as the men enter from the drawing-room.
They are* SIR JOHN FARINGFORD, *the* RECTOR, MR.
JACKSON, *and* HENRY.]

MR. JACKSON. Hullo, all alone, Lady Faringford?
What's become of Maria—and Mrs. Pratt?

VIOLET [*breaking off in the middle of her playing and
rising from the piano*]. Simmonds came to ask if he
could see Mrs. Pratt. Mrs. Simmonds is ill. Mother
and Mrs. Pratt are putting some things together for
him to take to her.

LADY FARINGFORD [*sweetly*]. Your daughter has
been entertaining us with her charming music while
Mrs. Jackson was away. What was that little piece
you were playing, dear?

VIOLET. A sonata of Beethoven, Lady Faringford.

LADY FARINGFORD. Indeed? Very pretty.

THE RECTOR. You are going to play at our next
Parish concert, I hope, Miss Jackson?

VIOLET. Yes. Mrs. Pratt and I have been getting
out the programme.

SIR JOHN. Miss Jackson is a tower of strength in
the musical line. Stella hardly plays a note. I

always tell my wife it's the result of having had a German governess. How can you expect a child to learn music in German ?

LADY FARINGFORD. I believe all modern music is written in German. It certainly sounds like it.

HENRY [*joining* STELLA, *who has made her escape from her mother to the other side of the room at the first opportunity*]. I hope you haven't been dull, Miss Faringford, while my mother has been out of the room. It's shocking of her to leave her guests in this way.

STELLA. Not at all. Vi has been playing to us. It has been delightful.

HENRY. You're very fond of music, aren't you ?

STELLA. Yes. It's curious, when I was a child they made me learn, of course, but I didn't care a bit about it. I was awfully troublesome over my lessons, I remember. So I made nothing of it. And now, when I'd give anything to be able to play, I can't.

HENRY. Why don't you take it up again ?

STELLA. I do try sometimes. Sometimes I set to work and practise feverishly for a whole week. But it doesn't last.

HENRY. You should persevere.

STELLA. I know, but I don't. I suppose I'm lazy. But that's like me. I want to do things. I see I *ought* to do them. But somehow they don't get done. I expect you can't understand that ?

HENRY. I'm afraid I can't. If I want a thing I take the necessary steps to get it. That's what " wanting " means with me.

STELLA [*thoughtfully*]. And do you always get it ?

HENRY. Generally. A man can generally get a thing in the end if he gives his mind to it.

STELLA. Most people wouldn't say that.

HENRY. That's because most people don't know what they want. Instead of fixing their mind on one thing, and being determined to get it, they keep aiming first at one thing and then at another. So of course they don't get anything. They don't deserve to.

STELLA [*rather wistfully*]. Most people don't *aim* at all. They simply take what comes.

HENRY. Surely *you* don't do that?

STELLA. I believe I do. [*Laughing.*] You see, there's really not room for more than one *will* in any family. In our family it's mamma's. Mamma always knows what she wants—like you. The worst of it is she doesn't always know what *we* want.

HENRY. I see. What happens then?

STELLA. Oh, mamma wins. We struggle a little sometimes, papa and I. But she gets her way in the end.

[*There is silence between them for a moment. HENRY looks round, and, noticing everybody else immersed in conversation, feels that his opportunity has come for laying his hand and heart at MISS FARINGFORD's feet. He drops his voice to a confidential undertone and sets about it.*]

HENRY. Miss Faringford, there's something I want to say to you.

STELLA. That sounds very serious.

HENRY. It is serious—to me. It's something I've wanted to tell you for a long time.

STELLA [*rising nervously*]. Well, don't tell it me to-night. Later on, perhaps. I don't think I want to hear about serious things to-night.

HENRY [*rising also*]. When may I tell it to you ?

STELLA. I don't know. Some time, perhaps. But not now. Here's your mother come back with Mrs. Pratt.

[*At this opportune moment* MRS. JACKSON *and* MRS. PRATT *do, as a matter of fact, re-enter from their ministrations to poor* SIMMONDS, *and* STELLA, *for the moment, is saved. She goes towards them.*]

MRS. JACKSON. Lady Faringford, what will you think of me for leaving you for so long ? But the housekeeper was out. She had gone down to the village to see her niece, who is ill. So Mrs. Pratt and I had to put the things together for Simmonds ourselves. Mrs. Simmonds has another baby, Samuel.

MRS. PRATT. The poor are terribly thoughtless in these matters. That makes her sixth. But I'm bound to say poor Simmonds seemed quite conscious of his folly.

LADY FARINGFORD. That, at least, is satisfactory. But I have no hope that it will affect his future conduct. He will go on having children—at the usual intervals—until he dies. And then they will all come on the parish.

MRS. JACKSON [*puzzled*]. But is Simmonds going to die ? He said nothing about it. But, of course, he was rather flurried.

MR. JACKSON [*staggered for the moment by the*

fatuity of his wife's remark, but recovering himself gamely]. I hope you sent whatever was necessary, Maria ?

MRS. PRATT. Far more. I really had to inter-fere to prevent Mrs. Jackson from emptying her store cupboard.

THE RECTOR. Well, well, I dare say poor Mrs. Simmonds will find a use for everything.

MR. JACKSON. No doubt. And besides, with an election in prospect——

SIR JOHN. Exactly ; it can do no harm.

MR. JACKSON. By the way, Sir John, as chairman of my election committee, there's a point on which I want your advice. The local branch of the Inde-pendent Order of Good Templars wrote to me ten days ago asking for a subscription. So I sent five guineas.

SIR JOHN. Quite right. The Temperance Vote must be reckoned with in this Division.

MR. JACKSON. Just so. But the Good Templars published the fact in the local newspaper.

SIR JOHN. Well, that's what you wanted, wasn't it ?

MR. JACKSON. Ye-es. No doubt. But I forgot that the Secretary of the local branch of the Licensed Victuallers' Association would be sure to see the paragraph, and write to me for an explanation.

SIR JOHN. I see. Did he ?

MR. JACKSON. Yes.

SIR JOHN. Ah ! What did you do ?

MR. JACKSON. I was in some doubt. But Sims, my agent, told me the Licensed Victuallers had a

Benevolent Fund or something. So I sent ten
guineas to that. That seemed the best way out of
the difficulty.

SIR JOHN. Much the best, much the best.
[*Trying to escape.*

MR. JACKSON [*detaining him*]. But that's not the
end of the matter. For now the Good Templars
have written to ask if I am prepared to support any
legislation designed to combat the evil of the Drink
Traffic. And the Licensed Victuallers want to know
if I will pledge myself to oppose any Bill which
aims at the reduction of the sale of intoxicating
liquors.

SIR JOHN. Hum! They rather had you
there!

MR. JACKSON. Yes. . . . However, I think
I've got out of it all right. I've written a letter to
the Licensed Victuallers to say I'm not in favour of
unduly restricting the sale of liquor in the interests
of Temperance Propaganda. And I've written
another to the Good Templars saying that I'm quite
in favour of Temperance Propaganda providing it
doesn't unduly restrict the sale of intoxicating liquor.
I think that meets the case?

SIR JOHN. I see. Running with the hare and
hunting with the hounds, eh? Quite right. I
think you got out of it very well. And now we
really must be saying good-night. [*To* LADY
FARINGFORD.] Come, my dear, it's time we were
going.

MRS. JACKSON. Oh, you mustn't go yet. It's
quite early.

LADY FARINGFORD. We are early people. [*Rises.*]

We really must go. Stella, my dear, we must be putting on our things.

HENRY. I'll ask if your carriage is round.

[*Rings.*

LADY FARINGFORD. If you will be so good. I told the coachman ten. I do hope it's stopped raining. I believe the farmers want it, but it's so bad for the horses.

HENRY [*to* BAINES, *who appears in answer to his ring*]. Lady Faringford's carriage.

BAINES. It's at the door, sir.

HENRY. Very well. [*Exit* BAINES.

LADY FARINGFORD. Good-night, then, Mrs. Jackson. Such a *pleasant* evening. Come, Stella.

[*General adieux. The* FARINGFORDS *and* STELLA *go out escorted by* HENRY *and* MR. JACKSON.]

MRS. PRATT. I think *we* ought to be going, too.

MRS. JACKSON. No, no. You mustn't run away like that. I've not had a moment to speak to the Rector. And I'm sure Vi will want to talk to you about the next concert. Sit down again, Mrs. Pratt. [*Re-enter* HENRY *and* MR. JACKSON.] What sort of a night is it, Samuel? Has it stopped raining? [*Sits down beside the* RECTOR *on the sofa.*

MR. JACKSON. Yes; it's not raining now. But it's very dark.

THE RECTOR. The moon's full, too. But I suppose there's too much cloud about.

MRS. JACKSON. I do hope it will be lighter before you have to go home. It's such a dark road from here to the Rectory.

THE RECTOR. We have a lantern. We always bring it when we go out at night. We don't trust the moon. She's fickle, Mrs. Jackson, like all her sex.

MRS. JACKSON. Rector, if you talk like that I shall scold you. And so will Mrs. Pratt.

[*There is a sudden noise of footsteps outside. Then the door opens hurriedly, and* BAINES *appears. He crosses at once to* MR. JACKSON, *and speaks in a sort of breathless undertone.*]

BAINES. If you please, Sir——

MR. JACKSON. Well, what is it, Baines ?

BAINES. If you please, Sir, it's . . . [*confidentially*] Mr. Eustace. [MR. JACKSON *turns sharply round.*] He was lying just by the front door.

MR. JACKSON. Mr. Eustace ?

MRS. JACKSON [*hearing the name and jumping up from her seat*]. Eustace !

BAINES. Yes, Sir. Yes, Madam. Thomas saw him just as he was coming in after shutting the front gate. The moon came out for a moment and he saw him. He's fainted, Sir. At least, I think so.

MRS. JACKSON. I must go to him.

[*Hurries towards door.*

MR. JACKSON. No. Not you, Maria. I'll go.

[*The door opens.*

BAINES. I think they're bringing him in here, Sir.

[*Enter the* TWO FOOTMEN, *carrying a draggled and dishevelled body by the shoulders and the heels. The room becomes a scene of excitement and confusion, everybody talking at once and getting into each other's way. Chairs are pushed this way and that, and the sofa is dragged out into the middle of the room to receive the body as it is brought in.*]

MRS. JACKSON. Oh, my poor boy ! My poor dear boy ! [*Rushes to him.*

VIOLET. Wait a minute. Put him here.

MRS. JACKSON. Oh, he's dead ! He's dead ! I know he's dead.

VIOLET. Hush, mother. Some brandy, quick, Baines. And some cold water. I think he's only fainted.

[*Puts cushion under his head and opens shirt at neck.*]

THE RECTOR. Poor fellow !

MRS. PRATT [*noticing the condition of* EUSTACE'S *boots*]. Oh, Mrs. Jackson. Your sofa ! It will be utterly ruined.

MRS. JACKSON [*bending over him, wild with anxiety*]. Oh, I wish they'd be quick with the brandy. Henry, go at once for Dr. Glaisher.

THE RECTOR. Let *me* go. We pass his house anyway. And we mustn't stay any longer. We should only be in the way here. Come, my dear.

Enter BAINES *with brandy and jug of water.*

MRS. PRATT. Good-bye, dear Mrs. Jackson. No. You mustn't stir. And I do hope he'll be all right soon. We'll send Dr. Glaisher round at once.

THE RECTOR. Good-bye. [*To* HENRY.] Don't come with me, my dear fellow. Baines can find my things. Stay and look after your brother.

[THE RECTOR *and* MRS. PRATT *flurry out, followed by* BAINES. *Meantime* MRS. JACKSON *has been trying to force some brandy between the clenched teeth of the patient.*]

VIOLET. Your handkerchief, Henry. Quick.

[HENRY *gives it to her. She dips it in jug, wrings it out and, kneeling beside the sofa, puts it over patient's forehead by way of bandage.*]

MRS. JACKSON [*lamentably*]. He doesn't stir.

MR. JACKSON. I can feel his heart beating a little, I think. But I'm not sure.

MRS. JACKSON. Oh, will he *never* come round ! I *wish* Dr. Glaisher would come. If he were to die !

VIOLET [*soothing her*]. Hush, mother. He's only fainted. Didn't you hear father say he could hear his heart beating ?

MRS. JACKSON. Is there anything else we could do ? My salts !

VIOLET [*rising*]. I'll get them, mother.

MRS. JACKSON. They're on my dressing-table. [VIOLET *nods and goes out quickly.*] . . . No, I remember I had them in the library this morning. I'll go and look. Or was it the breakfast-room ? I'm not sure. Oh dear, oh dear, poor darling Eustace !

[*And the poor old lady waddles out in a burst of tears.*]

MR. JACKSON. She'll never find them. You go, Henry, and help her. Try the breakfast-room.

[HENRY *goes out after his mother, and* MR. JACKSON *is left alone with his prostrate son. For a minute or so he fusses round, making futile and rather grotesque efforts to restore him to consciousness, re-moistening the bandage on his forehead and renewing the attempt to administer brandy. Then* VIOLET'S *voice is heard through the door, which is left open.*]

VIOLET [*without*]. Father !
MR. JACKSON [*going to door, hurriedly*]. Yes, yes, what *is* it ?

Enter VIOLET.

VIOLET. Have you your keys ? Mother thinks she may have left her salts on your desk in the library, and it's locked.
MR. JACKSON [*frantic with nervous irritation*]. Tck ! Here they are. [VIOLET *going.*] I'd better come or you'll disturb all my papers.

[MR. JACKSON *fusses out after his daughter, and for a minute or so the patient is left alone. The patient takes advantage of this to raise himself cautiously from his recumbent posture and wring out the bandage on his forehead, which he finds disagreeably wet. He also removes a novel with a bright red cover, inconsiderately left on the sofa, which somewhat interfered with his comfort as he lay upon it. He reads the title on the back of it, which is " Hester's Escape," and smiles*]

ACT I   139

grimly at his sister's taste in fiction. Hearing noise of returning footsteps, he hurriedly replaces the book on the sofa and the bandage on his forehead, and resumes his fainting condition as his mother re-enters with HENRY.]

MRS. JACKSON [*piteously*]. They're *not* in the library. Where *can* I have put them ?

HENRY. The others will find them. Violet is looking in your bedroom. She always finds things. And the governor is in the breakfast-room. They'll be here in a moment.

Enter VIOLET *with salts in her hand, followed at a short interval by* MR. JACKSON.

MRS. JACKSON. Thanks, dear. [*Bending over the patient and holding the salts tremulously to his nose, but entirely forgetting to take out the stopper.*] Where were they ?

VIOLET. In the dining-room, on the writing-table.

MRS. JACKSON. Oh yes, I remember. I had them there at lunch time. I *knew* I had put them somewhere.

HENRY [*irritably*]. There's no use holding those salts to his nose unless you take out the stopper, mother.

[MRS. JACKSON *fumbles with stopper. Patient stirs slightly and turns away his head.*]

MR. JACKSON. He's coming round. He moved a little. Try him with some more brandy.

[MRS. JACKSON *puts down salts and takes up brandy, which she pours into patient's mouth. He chokes a little, heaves a realistic sigh of returning consciousness, opens his eyes, then raises himself and looks round.*]

EUSTACE [*faintly*].   Is that you, mother ?
MRS. JACKSON [*overjoyed*].   Yes, dear, yes.
EUSTACE [*closing his eyes again*].   Where am I ?
MRS. JACKSON.   At home, dear.   Your own home. Oh, he's not dead !   He's not dead !

[*Embraces him, sobbing passionately as the curtain falls.*]

ACT II

SCENE:—*The breakfast-room at the* JACKSONS'. *A round breakfast-table occupies the centre of the stage, laid with cloth, tea and coffee things, and various dishes. The fireplace is on the left, and on either side of it are leather-covered arm-chairs. There is a large French window, open, at the back of the stage, through which is seen the garden bathed in summer sunshine. A door on the left leads to the hall. A night has passed since the Prodigal's return.* MR. JACKSON, HENRY, *and* VIOLET *are at breakfast,* VIOLET *having charge of the coffee,* MR. JACKSON *of the bacon dish.* HENRY *is reading "The Gloucester Chronicle" in the intervals of eating his bacon.* VIOLET *is reading letters.*]

HENRY [*holding out cup*]. More coffee, please, Violet. [*To* MR. JACKSON.] Wenhams have failed, father.

MR. JACKSON. It's only what we expected, isn't it ?

HENRY. Yes. Forty thousand they say here. But, of course, it's only a guess. No one can know till the accounts are made up.

MR. JACKSON. They've been shaky for some time. Well, how is he ?

[*This to* MRS. JACKSON, *who enters at this moment from hall. She has quite recovered her normal placidity,*

*and bears no resemblance to the tragic, tear-stained old
lady whom we last saw.*]

MRS. JACKSON. Much better. He looks quite a
different person.

MR. JACKSON. Did he eat any breakfast?

MRS. JACKSON. He hasn't had any yet. At least,
only a cup of tea. He says he'd rather come down.
He's getting up now.

VIOLET. Didn't Dr. Glaisher say he was to stay
in bed?

MRS. JACKSON. Yes. But if he wants to come
down I don't think it can do any harm. He can lie
down on the sofa till lunch if he feels tired.

MR. JACKSON. What time is Glaisher coming?

VIOLET. Half-past ten, he said.

HENRY. Has Eustace explained how he came to
be lying in the drive in that state? Last night we
could get nothing out of him.

MRS. JACKSON. No wonder. He was dazed, poor
boy. He had walked all the way from London, and
had had nothing to eat.

HENRY [*irritably*]. How was it he was *in* London?
He was sent to Australia.

MRS. JACKSON. He *had* been in Australia. He
worked his passage home.

MR. JACKSON. His money is all gone, I suppose—
the thousand pounds I gave him?

MRS. JACKSON [*placidly*]. I don't know, Samuel.
I didn't ask.

MR. JACKSON. Humph! . . . [*Pause.*] I'll
trouble you for the toast, please, Henry.

HENRY. I suppose we'd better make inquiries
about Wenhams, father? It might be worth our

while to buy the mill if it goes cheap. Then we could run it and ours together.

MR. JACKSON. Just so. Will you see to that ?

[HENRY *nods.*

MRS. JACKSON. I've got a letter to Aunt Isabel to send by the early post. I ought to have written it last night. Will you put it into the box for me, Samuel, as you go to the mill ?

MR. JACKSON. Certainly, my dear.

[MRS. JACKSON *goes to writing-table and writes her letter.*]

HENRY [*to his father*]. Very tiresome Eustace turning up in that disreputable condition last night. What will Stella think ?

MR. JACKSON. It's lucky the Faringfords had gone before he was brought in.

HENRY. The Pratts hadn't. Mrs. Pratt will have told the entire village before lunch time.

VIOLET. I don't see why we should mind if she does. There's nothing to be ashamed of.

[*Rising and going over to fireplace, having finished her breakfast.*]

HENRY [*impatiently*]. Well, we won't discuss it.

[*Returns to his paper.*

MR. JACKSON [*moving towards* HENRY, *and speaking in an undertone*]. By the way, Henry, did you say anything to Stella last night ?

HENRY [*hesitates*]. No.

MR. JACKSON. I thought you were going to.

HENRY. I was. In fact, I did begin. But she didn't let me finish. I suppose she didn't understand what I was going to say.

MR. JACKSON. Don't put it off too long. There may be an election any day now, and the Faringford influence means a great deal.

HENRY. You've got Faringford's influence already. He's chairman of your Committee.

MR. JACKSON. That's true. Still, he'll take more trouble when I'm one of the family, so to speak. Yes, I shouldn't put it off if I were you.

HENRY. Very well, father.

MR. JACKSON. Of course, Faringford is as poor as Job. The estate's mortgaged up to the hilt. And anything there is after he and Lady Faringford go out of the coach—if there is anything—will go to the son. Stella won't have a sixpence. Still, they're good people—position in the county and all that. And *you'll* have enough money for both.

HENRY. Yes. Especially if we get hold of Wenhams' mill. I'm sure I could make a good thing out of that. We'd put in turbines as we did here, get new machinery, and double our output.

MR. JACKSON. How are the turbines working, by the way?

HENRY. All right. And they'll go still better when the new sluices are done. [*Rising.*] Well, I shall go over to the mill now. Are you coming?

MR. JACKSON. In a moment.

[*Finishes his coffee and rises.*

VIOLET. Shall I get your hat and stick, father?

MR. JACKSON. Do, dear. [VIOLET *goes out in quest of these.*] Is your letter ready, Maria?

MRS. JACKSON. Just done. [*Fastens it up, rising.*] You won't forget it, will you?

MR. JACKSON. No. Or, if I do, Henry will remind me.

MRS. JACKSON [to HENRY, *who has collected his hat and papers, and is about to start for the mill*]. Won't you wait and see Eustace before you go, Henry? He'll be down in a moment.

HENRY. It doesn't matter. I shall see him soon enough. Coming, father?

[*Goes out by French window, crosses the lawn, and disappears.*]

MRS. JACKSON. I wish Henry could have stayed to see Eustace before he started.

MR. JACKSON. I dare say he'll be over in the course of the morning.

VIOLET [*re-entering*]. Here're your hat and stick, father.

MR. JACKSON. That's a good girl. [*Kisses her.*] Good-bye. I shall be in for lunch.

[*Goes out by French window, following* HENRY.

MRS. JACKSON [*going to bacon dish and lifting cover*]. We must order some more bacon. Or do you think Eustace had better have an egg?

VIOLET. Shall I go up and ask him?

MRS. JACKSON. Do, dear. And I wonder if you'd see cook at the same time and ask her if she's wanting anything? I have to go into the village.

VIOLET. Very well, mother.

[VIOLET *goes out on these errands.* MRS. JACKSON *takes away plates to sideboard, clears a place for* EUSTACE *where* HENRY *sat, and lays for him.*]

FOOTMAN [*announcing*]. Dr. Glaisher.

The Return of the Prodigal

[DR. GLAISHER *enters, very fussy and self-important, a worthy, seedy little man, who has long since forgotten all the medicine he ever knew.*]

MRS. JACKSON [*shaking hands*]. Oh, Doctor. Good morning. [*To* FOOTMAN.] Tell Mr. Eustace Dr. Glaisher is here. [FOOTMAN *goes out.*

DR. GLAISHER [*drawing off gloves in his best professional manner, and dropping them one after the other into his silk hat, which he has placed on the table*]. Well, how does he seem ? Going on well ?

MRS. JACKSON. Quite well, I think.

DR. GLAISHER. Did he have a good night ?

MRS. JACKSON. Excellent, he says.

DR. GLAISHER. Ah ! [*Nods sagely.*] Just so. Shall I go up to him ?

MRS. JACKSON. He's coming down for breakfast. He'll be here in a moment.

DR. GLAISHER. Coming down, is he ? Come, that looks satisfactory ! Still, we must be careful. No over-fatigue ! His condition last night gave cause for considerable anxiety. Indeed, I may say that if I had not fortunately been sent for at once and applied the necessary remedies, there was distinct danger of collapse—um ! distinct danger.

MRS. JACKSON. Oh, Doctor !

[*With singular want of tact,* EUSTACE *elects to enter at this moment, looking in quite robust health, and wearing an admirable suit of clothes.*]

DR. GLAISHER. Ah, here he is.

EUSTACE [*cheerily*]. Good morning, mother. [*Kisses her.*] Hullo, Doctor. Come to see me ?

DR. GLAISHER [*shaking hands*].   Well, and how are we this morning ?

EUSTACE.   Getting on all right, I think.   A bit limp and washed-out perhaps.

DR. GLAISHER.   Just so.   The temperature normal ?   No fever ?   [*Touches forehead.*]   That's right. Pulse ?   [*Feels it.*]   A little irregular, perhaps.   But nothing serious.   Excitement due to over-fatigue, no doubt.   Now let me see your tongue.   [*Does so. Nods sagely.*]   Just so.   As I should have expected. *Just* as I should have expected, dear Mrs. Jackson. Appetite not very good, I suppose ?

EUSTACE.   Er—not very.

DR. GLAISHER.   Just so.   Just so.
[*Nods more sagaciously than ever.*

EUSTACE [*gaily*].   Not dead yet, eh, Doctor ?

MRS. JACKSON.   My dear !

DR. GLAISHER [*with heavy geniality*].   We shall pull you through.   Oh, we shall pull you through. But you must take care of yourself for a few days. No excitement !   No over-fatigue.   The system wants *tone* a little, wants *tone*.

EUSTACE.   I see.   I'm to take it easy, in fact, for a bit, eh ?

DR. GLAISHER.   Just so.

EUSTACE.   I won't forget.   I say, what clever beggars you doctors are !   You feel a fellow's pulse and look at his tongue, and you know *all* about him at once.   Don't you ?

DR. GLAISHER [*pleased*].   Not *all* perhaps.   But there are indications, symptoms, which the professional man can interpret . . .

EUSTACE [*interrupting*].   Quite extraordinary.   I

say, what do you think of these clothes ? Not bad, are they ? They're Henry's. But *I* chose them—out of his wardrobe. Poor old Henry !

MRS. JACKSON. How naughty of you, Eustace. I'm sure Henry won't like it.

EUSTACE. Of course he won't, mother dear. Nobody does like his clothes being worn by some one else. But I must wear something, you know. I can't come down to breakfast in a suit of pyjamas. Besides, they're Henry's pyjamas.

MRS. JACKSON. But I told Thomas specially to put out an old suit of your father's for you. Didn't he do it ?

EUSTACE. Yes. But I can't wear the governor's clothes, you know. We haven't the same figure. I say, I'd better ring for breakfast. [*Does so.*

MRS. JACKSON. Have you ordered it, dear ? I sent Vi up to ask whether you'd like bacon or eggs.

EUSTACE. Yes. Violet asked me. I said bacon *and* eggs. Hullo, Vi, you're just in time to pour out my coffee.

[*This to* VIOLET, *who re-enters at this moment from interviewing the cook and otherwise attending to her mother's household duties.*]

DR. GLAISHER [*shakes hands with* VIOLET]. Well, I must be off to my other patients. [*To* MRS. JACKSON.] Good-bye, Mrs. Jackson. He is going on well—quite as well as can be expected, that is. There are no fresh symptoms of an unfavourable character. But you must keep him quiet for a few days. There are signs of nervousness about him, a sort of suppressed excitement, which I don't like.

The system wants *tone*, decidedly wants *tone*. I'll
send him up a mixture to take. He has evidently
been through some strain lately. I knew that
directly I saw him last night. You can't deceive a
doctor !

[MAN *brings in breakfast—rack of toast on table,*
coffee and rolls on sideboard.]

MRS. JACKSON (*anxiously*). You don't think
there's anything *serious* the matter ?

DR. GLAISHER. No ! no ! Let us hope not. The
general constitution is sound enough. Not over
strong perhaps, but sound. And with youth on his
side. Let me see, how old is he ?

MRS. JACKSON. Nine and twenty.

DR. GLAISHER [*taking refuge in his sage nod again*].
Just so. Just so. . . . [*Cheering up.*] Well, *good*
morning. [*To* EUSTACE.] *Good* morning. And remember, quiet, perfectly quiet. I'll look in again
to-morrow and see how he's getting on.

EUSTACE [*nods*]. Good-bye. [*Goes towards break-*
fast table, where the FOOTMAN *by now has placed*
coffee, toast, and bacon and eggs.]

[DR. GLAISHER *shakes hands with* VIOLET *and goes*
out, followed by FOOTMAN. VIOLET *seats herself at*
table to pour out EUSTACE's *coffee.* MRS. JACKSON
draws up a chair, and sits by his side with placid con-
tentment, watching him eat.]

EUSTACE [*beginning his breakfast*]. Mother, I
think I must become a doctor. It's the only profession I know of which seems to require no knowledge

whatever. And it's the sort of thing I should do rather well.

Mrs. Jackson. I dare say, dear. You must speak to your father about it. . . . And now you must tell us *all* about yourself. What have you been doing all this time? And why did you never write?

Eustace. There was nothing to tell you—that you'd have liked to hear.

Mrs. Jackson. My dear, of course we should have liked to hear everything about you.

Eustace. I doubt it. No news is good news. I bet the governor thought that—and Henry.

Mrs. Jackson. No, no, dear. I assure you your father was quite anxious when we never heard— at first.

Eustace. Ah, well, if the governor was so anxious to know how I was he shouldn't have packed me off to Australia. I never could endure writing letters.

Violet. Still, you might have sent us word. It would have been kinder to mother.

Eustace [*laying his hand on his mother's as it lies on the arm of her chair*]. Poor mother. I suppose I was a brute. But I've not been very prosperous these five years, and as I'd nothing pleasant to say I thought I wouldn't write.

Mrs. Jackson. But what became of your money, dear? The thousand pounds your father gave you?

Eustace. I lost it.

Mrs. Jackson [*looking round vaguely as if* Eustace *might have dropped it somewhere on the carpet, in which case, of course, it ought to be picked up before some one treads on it*]. Lost it?

EUSTACE. Yes. Part of it went in a sheep farm. I suppose I was a bad farmer. Anyhow, the sheep died. The other part I put in a gold mine. I suppose I wasn't much of a miner. Anyhow, there was no gold in it. I was in the Mounted Police for a time. That was in Natal. It wasn't bad, but it didn't lead to anything. So I cleared out. I've been in a bank at Hong-kong. I've driven a cable car in San Francisco. I've been a steward on a liner. I've been an actor, and I've been a journalist. I've tried my hand at most things, in fact. At one time I played in an orchestra.

MRS. JACKSON [*with fond pride*]. You were always fond of music.

EUSTACE [*dryly*]. Yes, I played the triangle—and took a whack at the big drum between times.

VIOLET. How absurd you are!

EUSTACE. Finally, I came home. That was when my experience as a steward came in. I worked my passage as one—if you can call it work! I was sick all the time.

MRS. JACKSON. How dreadful!

EUSTACE. It was—for the passengers.

VIOLET. How long ago was that?

EUSTACE. Only about a month. Since then I've been in London picking up a living one way or another. At last, when I found myself at the end of my tether, I started to walk here. And here I am.

MRS. JACKSON. My dear boy! You must have found it terribly muddy!

EUSTACE. I did. But life always is rather muddy, isn't it ? At least, that's my experience.

MRS. JACKSON. But weren't you *very* tired ?

EUSTACE. I was tired, of course. Give me some more coffee, Vi.

[*She does so.* EUSTACE *takes advantage of this to change the subject, gently but firmly.*]

Well, how have you all been at home ? How's the governor ?

MRS. JACKSON. He's been very well on the whole. His lumbago was rather troublesome at the end of last year. Otherwise he's been all right.

EUSTACE. Does he stick to business as close as ever ?

MRS. JACKSON. Not quite. You see, Henry's a partner now. The firm is Jackson, Hartopp, and Jackson, and *he* takes a good deal of work off your father's shoulders. Henry is an excellent man of business.

[EUSTACE *nods.*]

Your father gives more of his time to public affairs now. He's a magistrate, and been on the County Council for the last three years. And now he's standing for Parliament.

EUSTACE. The family's looking up in the world. The business is flourishing, then ?

MRS. JACKSON. Oh yes. They've put in all new machinery in the last three years. And they've got turbines instead of the old water-wheels. That was Henry's idea. And now they can turn out a cheaper cloth than any of the mills round here.

EUSTACE. Cheaper ? The governor used to despise cheap cloth.

MRS. JACKSON. Yes. But Henry said it was no use making cloth that would last a lifetime if people only wanted it to last twelve months. So he got over new machines—from America. And now they don't make any *good* cloth at all, and your father has trebled his income.

EUSTACE. Bravo, Henry !

MRS. JACKSON [*rises*]. And now I really must go down to the village and do my shopping. Have you got cook's list, Vi ?

VIOLET. Yes, mother. But I'm coming, too. I promised Mrs. Pratt I'd call at the Vicarage before twelve to arrange about the next Mothers' Meeting.

MRS. JACKSON [*to* EUSTACE]. You'll find the paper there, dear, and some cigarettes—unless you think you oughtn't to smoke ? I'll ring for them to clear away. And remember, dear [*kisses him gently on the forehead*] Dr. Glaisher said you were to keep *quite* quiet.

EUSTACE. All right, mother. I'll remember.

[MRS. JACKSON *and* VIOLET *go out to their shopping in the village.* EUSTACE, *who has risen to open the door for them, closes it, and returns slowly towards the table. The smile dies out of his face, and he gives a perceptible yawn. Then he chooses a cigarette, lights it in leisurely fashion, takes up a paper, selects an armchair by the fireplace, sits down, and begins to read. After a moment or two, enter* BAINES, *with a tray in his hand.*]

You can clear away, Baines.

BAINES.   Thank you, sir.

[*There is silence for an appreciable time, while* BAINES *goes on clearing the table. Then he speaks, but without pausing in his work.*]

I hope you're feeling better this morning, sir ?

EUSTACE.   Thanks, Baines, the doctor thinks I'm getting on all right.

BAINES.   Narrow escape you had last night, sir. Thomas says the carriage wheels must have gone within a foot of your head.

EUSTACE.   Thomas is a—I mean, does he say that ?

BAINES.   Curious thing we shouldn't have seen you, sir. We must have been that close ! But it was a very dark night except when the moon was out. Then it was as bright as day almost. That was how he came to see you, sir.

EUSTACE.   Oh, that was it, was it ?

BAINES.   Yes, sir. [*The subject interests him so much that for a moment he actually stops his clearing.*] You see, Thomas had just shut the gate after the carriage drove away and the moon happened to come out . . .

EUSTACE [*bored*].   Quite so.

[BAINES, *snubbed, resumes his work with dignity. After an interval* EUSTACE *speaks again.*]

Whose carriage was it, by the way ?

BAINES [*still offended*].   Sir John Faringford's, sir.

EUSTACE.   Well, if one's head is to be driven

ACT II   155 over, it may as well be by a member of the aristocracy. Eh, Baines?

BAINES [*refusing to be mollified*]. Certainly, sir.

EUSTACE. Sir John often dine here nowadays?

BAINES. Yes, sir. And Lady Faringford, and Miss Stella.

EUSTACE. Miss Stella?

BAINES [*thawing a little, but not sufficiently appeased to pause in his work again*]. Their daughter, sir. But I dare say you wouldn't remember her. Only came out about a year ago.

EUSTACE. So my father is standing for Parliament, is he?

BAINES. Yes, sir.

EUSTACE. Will he get in?

BAINES. It's thought so, sir.

EUSTACE. By the way, which side is he on?

BAINES [*puzzled*]. I beg pardon, sir?

EUSTACE. Which side? Liberal or Conservative?

BAINES. Conservative, *of course*, sir. All the people round here are Conservative. All the gentry, that is.

EUSTACE. Most respectable, eh, Baines?

BAINES. Yes, sir.

[BAINES, *who has tray in his hand, hears bell, has a moment of indecision, then puts tray down on table.*]

Excuse me, sir.

[BAINES *goes out to answer the bell.* EUSTACE *returns to his newspaper. After a minute or so* BAINES *returns, and wanders about the room looking for some-*

thing. Presently this proceeding gets on EUSTACE'S *nerves, and he looks up irritably.*]

EUSTACE. What is it, Baines? Do you want anything?

BAINES. If you please, sir, Miss Faringford has called for a book Miss Violet promised to lend her.

[*Continues to search.*
EUSTACE [*after pause*]. Have you found it?

BAINES. No, sir.

EUSTACE [*bored, putting down paper on other arm-chair, and rising*]. I suppose I'd better see her.

[*He goes out.* BAINES *folds tablecloth and puts it away in sideboard drawer. Is just about to go out carrying tray, when enter* STELLA, *followed by* EUSTACE. BAINES *draws back to let them pass, and then goes out and closes the door.*]

EUSTACE. Come in, Miss Faringford. Perhaps I can find the book for you. What was it like?

STELLA. It was just an ordinary looking novel with a bright red cover—called "Hester's Escape."

EUSTACE [*wandering round the room, looking on the various tables, and then glancing hopelessly at the book-shelves*]. "Hestor's Escape?" I seem to remember the name. But Vi will know where it is. You'd better wait till she comes in. Sit down. She'll be back directly.

[*This hospitable invitation is prompted partly by* EUSTACE'S *disinclination to search through those book-shelves, partly by his observing for the first time that*

STELLA *is a very pretty girl, a fact which had escaped his notice in the relative darkness of the hall.*]

STELLA. Are you sure ?

EUSTACE. Quite !

[STELLA *takes one of the arm-chairs by the fireplace.*]

You won't mind an untidy room, will you ? I'm afraid I breakfasted late.

STELLA. I wonder you are down at all.

EUSTACE. Oh, I'm all right.

[*Turns round one of the chairs at the breakfast-table and sits near her.*]

STELLA. Are you sure you ought to talk ? People who have been ill ought to be quiet, oughtn't they ?

EUSTACE. There's really nothing the matter with me.

STELLA. That's not what Mrs. Pratt told me. I met her in the village as I was coming here.

EUSTACE. Ah yes. She was present, of course, when I made my dramatic entry. Did she tell you about it ? I hope it went off well ?

STELLA. You frightened every one terribly, if that's what you mean. Mrs. Pratt says you looked *dreadful.* She thought you were going to die.

EUSTACE. Quite a thrilling experience for her. She ought to be very much obliged to me.

STELLA. How can you joke about it ? You might really have died, you know ! But when people have travelled all over the world as you have done, and endured hardship and danger, I suppose death doesn't seem so terrible to them as it does to us who stay at home ?

EUSTACE.   I suppose not.   They get used to it.

STELLA.   Have you often been in great danger ?
Really great, I mean ?

EUSTACE.   I was at Singapore when the plague
was there.

STELLA.   How awful !

EUSTACE.   Yes.   It wasn't pleasant.

STELLA.   I can't think how any one can stay in
England when he might go out and see the world.
[*Enthusiastic.*]   If I were a man I would go abroad
and visit strange countries, and have wonderful
adventures as you have done, not waste my life in a
dull little village like Chedleigh.

EUSTACE.   My dear Miss Faringford, the whole
world is a dull little village like Chedleigh, and
I've wasted my life in it.

Enter BAINES.

BAINES.   If you please, sir, the Rector has called
to ask how you are.

EUSTACE.   Oh, bother.   Say I'm very much
obliged and I'm all right.   [*Turns to* STELLA *again.*

BAINES.   He said he would like to see you if you
felt well enough, sir.

EUSTACE.   Ah ! wait a minute.   [*Thinks.*]   Will
you say I'm not well at all and quite unfit to see him
this morning ?

BAINES.   Very well, sir.   [BAINES *goes out.*

STELLA [*rising*].   And now I must go.   I'm only
tiring you, and I expect you oughtn't to talk.

EUSTACE.   But I assure you——

STELLA.   And as you're quite unfit to see
visitors——

EUSTACE. I'm quite unfit to see the Rector. That's a very different thing. But I'm perfectly up to seeing you. Besides Violet should be here directly, now. [*Persuasively.*] Sit down again.

STELLA [*hesitating*]. I don't think I *ought* to stay.

EUSTACE. I'm sure you ought. One should visit the sick, you know.

STELLA [*with a laugh*]. You don't seem quite able to make up your mind whether you're ill or well.

EUSTACE. No. I vary. I find it more convenient.

Re-enter BAINES.

Well, who is it *now*, Baines ?

BAINES. Lady Faringford.

[BAINES's *remark is not a reply to* EUSTACE's *question, nor yet a rebuke to his irritability, though it sounds not unlike the latter. He is merely announcing a visitor with his usual impassive dignity. The announcement almost startles* STELLA *out of her self-control, and she rises hastily.* EUSTACE *is less impressed, as he has not yet made the acquaintance of* LADY FARINGFORD, *and is merely bored at being interrupted, but he also rises.*]

STELLA. Mamma !

LADY FARINGFORD [*ignoring her*]. Mr. Eustace Jackson, is it not ? How do you do ? [*Shakes hands frigidly.*] I heard in the village of your sudden return, and stopped the carriage to ask how you were. As the servant told me you were downstairs, I thought I would come in for a moment.

EUSTACE. Very kind of you, Lady Faringford.

LADY FARINGFORD [*severely*]. You hardly appear as ill as I expected.

EUSTACE [*genially, quite refusing to be snubbed*]. I hope the disappointment is an agreeable one ?

LADY FARINGFORD. *No* disappointments are agreeable, sir. [*Turning sternly to her daughter.*] And pray, what are *you* doing here, Stella ?

EUSTACE [*still maddeningly genial*]. Miss Faringford called for a book my sister lent her last night, "Hester's Escape." I persuaded her to come in and sit down till Violet returned.

LADY FARINGFORD. You are expecting her soon ?

EUSTACE. Every moment.

LADY FARINGFORD. Ah ! Then I don't think we can wait.

EUSTACE. But Miss Faringford's book. . . . She mustn't go away without it. Sit down for a moment while I see if I can find it. [*To* STELLA.] A bright red cover, I think you said ?

[*Looks round the room for it.*

LADY FARINGFORD [*icily*]. Pray don't trouble, Mr. Jackson.

EUSTACE. "Hester's Escape " ? I'm sure I've seen it somewhere. [*Thinks a moment.*] I know ! It was in the drawing-room last night. Excuse me for a moment. I'll go and get it.

[EUSTACE *goes out in quest of the book, which indeed is the very one which interfered with his comfort on the sofa the previous evening. The moment he has left the room,* LADY FARINGFORD *turns wrathfully on her daughter.*]

ACT II   I : L   161

LADY FARINGFORD.   Really, Stella, I'm surprised at you !

STELLA.   What is it, mamma ?

LADY FARINGFORD.   You know perfectly well. How long have you been here ?

STELLA.   About ten minutes.   A quarter of an hour, perhaps.

LADY FARINGFORD.   Do you make a habit of paying morning calls upon young men without a chaperon ?

STELLA.   No, mamma.

LADY FARINGFORD.   Then I hope you will not begin to do so.

STELLA [*goaded by her tone to the nearest approach to rebellion of which she is capable*].   I came to call for a book which Vi promised to lend me.   Vi was out, and Mr. Jackson very kindly asked me to come in and wait.   What harm is there in that ?

LADY FARINGFORD.   There is every harm.   Understand, please, that Mr. Eustace Jackson is not a suitable acquaintance for you.

STELLA.   He is Henry's brother.   You have no objection to my knowing Henry.

LADY FARINGFORD.   That is quite different. Henry has a large income and excellent prospects.   He is a man whom any young girl may be allowed to know.   Eustace is a mere ne'er-do-well.

STELLA.   Am I never to speak to any one who isn't rich ?   The Du Cranes aren't rich, or the Vere-Anstruthers.   Yet we know them. · We aren't rich ourselves, if it comes to that.

LADY FARINGFORD. That has nothing to do with it. The Du Cranes and poor George Anstruther are gentlepeople. The Jacksons are tradesmen.

STELLA. I think people make far too much fuss about being " gentlepeople."

LADY FARINGFORD. Then I hope you won't say so. I don't like this pernicious modern jargon about shopkeepers and gentlefolk being much the same. There's far too much truth in it to be agreeable.

STELLA [obstinately]. If it's true why shouldn't we say it ?

LADY FARINGFORD. Because we have everything to lose by doing so. We were born into this world with what is called position. Owing to that position we are received everywhere, flattered, made much of. Though we are poor, rich people are eager to invite us to their houses and marry our daughters. So much the better for us. But if we began telling people that position was all moonshine, family an antiquated superstition, and many duchesses far less like ladies than their maids, the world would ultimately discover that what we were saying was perfectly true. Whereupon we should lose the very comfortable niche in the social system which we at present enjoy, and—who knows ?— might actually be reduced in the end to doing something useful for our living like other people. No, no, my dear, rank and birth and the peerage *may* be all nonsense, but it isn't *our* business to say so. Leave that to vulgar people who have something to gain by it. *Noblesse oblige !*

[*This luminous exposition of the* FARINGFORD *social creed has just reached its allotted end when* EUSTACE *re-enters with the missing book.*]

EUSTACE.   Here's the book, Miss Faringford.   I hope you haven't had to wait too long ?   It was in the drawing-room, as I thought, but it had got put away under some papers.

STELLA.   Thank you so much.

LADY FARINGFORD [*rising, icily*].   Good-bye, Mr. Jackson.

STELLA [*shaking hands with deafint cordiality*]. Good-bye.   Give my love to Violet.

[EUSTACE *opens the door for* LADY FARINGFORD *and her daughter, and follows them out politely to see them to their carriage.   A moment later* HENRY *is seen crossing the lawn.   He enters by the French window. He has some letters and other papers of a business character in his hand, which he puts down on writing table.   He takes off his hat, sits down, and begins to write a note.   Presently* EUSTACE *re-enters, but* HENRY *does not notice him as his back is turned to the door.*]

EUSTACE [*after contemplating his brother's back for a moment with a grim smile*].   Hullo, Henry. Where did you spring from ?

HENRY [*turning in his chair at the sound of his voice*].   From the mill.   I came across the lawn. We had a short cut made through the shrubbery and a gate put three years ago.   It's quicker.

EUSTACE.   One of *your* improvements, eh ?

HENRY.   Yes.   [EUSTACE *laughs genially.*]

You're amused ?

EUSTACE. It's so like you having a path made so as to get to your work quicker.

HENRY [*briefly*]. Yes. I'm not an idler.

EUSTACE. Quite so. And *I* am, you mean ?

HENRY [*shrugs*]. I didn't say so.

EUSTACE [*quite good-humoured*]. You wanted to spare my feelings, no doubt ? Very thoughtful of you.

HENRY [*after a pause*]. Is the mater in ?

EUSTACE. I believe not. [*Another pause.*] By the way, I've been borrowing some of your clothes. Not a bad fit, are they ? It's lucky we're so much the same size.

HENRY [*grimly*]. Very !

EUSTACE. It's particularly lucky, as I've been entertaining visitors on behalf of the family.

HENRY [*frigidly*]. Indeed ?

EUSTACE. Yes. One of them a very charming visitor.

HENRY [*not interested*]. Who was that ?

EUSTACE. Miss Faringford.

HENRY [*startled*]. Stella ?

EUSTACE. Yes. [*Easily.*] Very nice girl altogether. She was here quite a long time while I told her my adventures—or as much of them as I thought suitable. Then unhappily her mother turned up. Rather an awful woman that !

HENRY [*annoyed*]. What did Stella come for ?

EUSTACE [*chaffing him gently*]. Not to inquire after me, if that's what you mean. Miss Faringford came for a book Vi had lent her, "Hester's Escape." She's certainly a very pretty girl. And a nice one.

HENRY [*stiffly*]. I may as well tell you I intend to marry Stella Faringford.

EUSTACE. Indeed? [*Pause.*] Have you asked her yet?

HENRY [*snaps*]. No.

EUSTACE. Then I wouldn't be too sure if I were you. Perhaps she won't have you.

[*This suggestion is too much for* HENRY, *who rises sharply from his chair, gathering up his papers with a view to finishing his writing in another room. When he has got half-way to the door he suddenly recollects himself, and turns sharp round to his brother.*]

HENRY. Oh, by the way, how are you?

EUSTACE [*laughing*]. I'm all right, thanks.

HENRY [*irritably*]. How on earth did you come to be lying in the drive in that way last night?

EUSTACE [*airily*]. Exhaustion, my dear chap. Cold and exposure! Hunger! You know the kind of thing.

HENRY. Cold? Why, it's the height of summer.

EUSTACE [*shrugging his shoulders*]. Heat, then.

HENRY [*exasperated*]. But how did you manage to *get* there? That's what *I* want to know. You are supposed to be in Australia.

EUSTACE [*beginning to laugh*]. I'll tell you. Only you must promise not to give me away.

HENRY. Give you away?

EUSTACE. Yes. [*Pause. He plunges into his story.*] I was awfully hard up and awfully sick of finding jobs and losing them, and at last I began to long for a proper dinner, properly served, and a decent suit of clothes. Like these. I thought of

166   ACT II

writing to the governor, but that would have been no good. He'd have sent me some good advice and the mater would have sent a fiver, and in a fortnight things would have been as bad as ever. At last I thought of a dramatic *coup*. The Prodigal's Return! The Fatted Calf! A father softened, a mother in tears! The virtuous elder brother scowling in the background! So I came here. Back to the Old Home, you know. At the front door I selected a convenient spot and lay down in an elaborate faint. Excuse the pun. I chose the moment just after the Faringfords' carriage had gone. I knew the footman would have to come in after shutting the gate, and I intended to kick his leg and groan in an impressive manner. Anything to attract attention. Fortunately, the moon came out just at the right moment, so the fool couldn't help spotting me. He called Baines, who recognised me in a moment. They were very sympathetic. I expect they thought I was drunk. The lower classes are always sympathetic to intoxication. I was borne into the drawing-room, the wandering sheep returned to the fold, the exile home again. Tableau! Most pathetic!

HENRY [*disgusted*]. And so you *walked* all the way from London to Chedleigh in order to play off a heartless practical joke.

EUSTACE. Walked? Nonsense. I came by train.

HENRY. But you told Vi you walked.

EUSTACE. I said I *started* to walk. I only got as far as the station.

HENRY [*angrily*]. It was unpardonable. The mater was awfully upset. So was the governor.

EUSTACE. That was the idea. There's nothing like a sudden shock to bring out any one's real feelings. The governor had no idea how fond he was of me until he saw me apparently dead, and unlikely to give him further trouble. And by the time I came round he'd forgotten the cause of his sudden affection—or perhaps he's never realised it—and was genuinely glad to see me. Psychologically, it was most interesting.

HENRY. It was extremely undignified and quite unnecessary. If you had simply come up to the front door and rung the bell you would have been received just as readily.

EUSTACE. I doubt it. In fact, I doubt if I should have been received at all. I might possibly have been given a bed for the night, but only on the distinct understanding that I left early the next morning. Whereas now nobody talks of my going. A poor invalid! In the doctor's hands! Perfect quiet essential. No. My plan was best.

HENRY. Why didn't that fool Glaisher see through you ?

EUSTACE. Doctors never see through their patients. It's not what they're paid for, and it's contrary to professional etiquette.

[HENRY *snorts wrathfully.*]

Besides, Glaisher's an ass, I'm glad to say.

HENRY [*fuming*]. It would serve you right if I told the governor the whole story.

EUSTACE. I dare say. But you won't. It wouldn't be cricket. Besides, I only told you on condition you kept it to yourself.

HENRY [*indignant*]. And so *I'm* to be made a partner in *your* fraud. The thing's a swindle, and I've got to take a share in it.

EUSTACE. Swindle? Not a bit. You've lent a hand—without intending it—to reuniting a happy family circle. Smoothed the way for the Prodigal's return. A very beautiful trait in your character.

HENRY [*grumpy*]. What I don't understand is *why* you told me all this. Why in heaven's name didn't you keep the whole discreditable story to yourself?

EUSTACE [*with flattering candour*]. The fact is I was pretty sure *you'd* find me out. The governor's a perfect owl, but you've got brains—of a kind. You can see a thing when it's straight before your nose. So I thought I'd let you into the secret from the start, just to keep your mouth shut.

HENRY. Tck! [*Thinks for a moment.*] And what are you going to do now you *are* at home?

EUSTACE [*airily*]. *Do*, my dear chap? Why, nothing.

[*And on the spectacle of* EUSTACE'S *smiling self-assurance and* HENRY'S *outraged moral sense, the curtain falls.*]

ACT III

SCENE.—*The Lawn at Chedleigh Court. Ten days have passed since Act II. It is a Saturday, and the time is after luncheon. On the left stands the house, its French windows open on to the lawn. The lawn is bounded by a shrubbery, through which runs the path which* HENRY *had made three years previously to enable him to get to the mill quicker. When the curtain rises,* EUSTACE *is lying in a hammock, swinging lazily. He wears a new grey flannel suit, and looks exceedingly comfortable. Hard by, under a tree, are three or four wicker chairs, in one of which* HENRY *is sitting, reading the Market Report in " The Times."* EUSTACE *has a cup of coffee in his hand.* HENRY *has one on table beside him. Presently* EUSTACE *drinks some, looking with indolent amusement at his brother absorbed in his news-paper.*

EUSTACE.   Not bad coffee, this.   [*Finishes it, and begins to perform the acrobatic feat of putting his cup and saucer on to the ground without falling out of the hammock.*]

HENRY [*looking up*].   I dare say.   [*Drinks some.*] You'll drop that cup.

EUSTACE.   I think not.   [*Puts cup on to ground, and resumes his recumbent posture indolently.*]

HENRY. If you leave it there some one's sure to put his foot in it.

EUSTACE. I'll risk it.

HENRY. *Bah !*

[*Rises, and puts* EUSTACE'S *cup on table.*

EUSTACE. Thanks, my dear chap. Perhaps it *is* safer there.

[HENRY *grunts again and returns to his newspaper.* EUSTACE *gets cigarette out of pocket and lights it in a leisurely manner.*]

Anything exciting in the paper ? Any convulsions in Wool ?

HENRY [*snaps*]. No !

EUSTACE. Where's the governor ? He generally comes home to luncheon on Saturdays, doesn't he ?

HENRY. He's lunching at the Wilmingtons' with the mater. He'll be back soon. There's a meeting of his Election Committee at four.

EUSTACE. Where ?

HENRY. Here.

EUSTACE. Will he get in ?

HENRY. Faringford thinks so. But it'll be a close thing. A very little might turn the scale either way.

EUSTACE. Cost him a good deal, I suppose ?

HENRY. Pretty well.

EUSTACE. *Panem et Circenses,* bread and circuses. That's the Tory prescription, isn't it ? Particularly circuses.

HENRY. I dare say.

Enter BAINES.

BAINES. Dr. Glaisher to see you, sir.

[THE DOCTOR *comes out of the house and advances briskly to his patient.* BAINES *collects coffee cups and exit.*]

EUSTACE [*stretching out hand from hammock*]. How do you do, Doctor? I'm following your prescription, you see. Rest! Rest! There's nothing like it.

DR. GLAISHER [*with a sagacious nod*]. Just so. I really came for your father's committee. I thought it was to be at three o'clock. But your man tells me it's not till four. So I thought I'd take a look at my patient. Well, and how are we to-day?

[*During this scene* HENRY *almost chokes with indignation.* EUSTACE *enjoys himself immensely.*]

EUSTACE. Going on all right, thanks. Still a little limp perhaps.

DR. GLAISHER. Just so. The temperature normal? No fever? That's right. [*Feels pulse.*] Pulse quite regular? Now the tongue. Just so. As I should have expected. *Just* as I should have expected. Appetite still good?

EUSTACE. Excellent, thanks.

DR. GLAISHER. You're still taking your glass of port at eleven? Just so. Oh, you'll soon be all right.

EUSTACE. Thanks to *you*, Doctor.

DR. GLAISHER. Not at all. *Not* at all. [*To* HENRY.] He'll soon be himself again now. System still wants *tone* a little, wants *tone*. I'll send him round some more of that mixture. Otherwise he's all right. [HENRY *grunts.*

EUSTACE. And you'll look in again in a day or two just to see how I am, won't you, Doctor ?

DR. GLAISHER. Certainly, if you wish it. And now I must be off. I have a couple of patients near here whom I can see in the next half-hour and be back again by four. Good-bye. Good-bye. Don't disturb yourself, pray.

[*To* HENRY, *who pays not the smallest attention to him.* THE DOCTOR *fusses off into the house.*]

HENRY [*savagely*]. Ass !

EUSTACE. My dear chap !

HENRY. Old Glaisher is a perfect noodle.

EUSTACE. Naturally. How much does a little country doctor make hereabouts ? Four hundred a year ? Say four hundred and fifty. You can't expect a first-rate intellect for that. 'Tisn't the market rate.

HENRY. I don't expect an absolute idiot.

EUSTACE. Glaisher doesn't *know* anything, of course, but his manner's magnificently impressive. After he's talked to me for five minutes, felt my pulse, and looked at my tongue, I almost begin to wonder whether I'm not really ill after all. That's a great gift for a doctor !

HENRY. You're perfectly well. Any fool can see that merely by looking at you. And old Glaisher goes on with his mixture and his glass of port at eleven. Bah ! [EUSTACE *laughs.*] And you encourage him. How many visits has he paid you ?

EUSTACE. I don't know. Seven or eight.

HENRY. And every one of them completely unnecessary.

EUSTACE. Completely unnecessary for me, but

very useful to old Glaisher, considering they mean half a guinea a piece to him.

HENRY. Which the governor pays.

EUSTACE. Which the governor pays, as you say. That's why I do it. Somebody must keep old Glaisher going, or what would become of all the little Glaishers? Here's the governor, with piles of money to throw away on Parliamentary elections and similar tomfoolery. Why shouldn't I divert some of it to old Glaisher. I like the little man.

HENRY. You're awfully generous—with other people's money.

EUSTACE. I am. Whose money are *you* generous with?

[HENRY *snorts with disapproval. Further discussion, however, is prevented by the appearance of* MR. *and* MRS. JACKSON, *who come out of the house at this moment. They are in their best apparel, having just returned from their luncheon party.*]

EUSTACE. Morning, father. I've not seen you before to-day. You went out before I got down.

MR. JACKSON [*gruffly, sitting down*]. Good morning.

EUSTACE. Morning, mummy.

[MRS. JACKSON *kisses him affectionately, then seats herself in one of the chairs. He turns to his father again.*]

By the way, you've just missed one of your Election Committee.

MR. JACKSON [*alarmed*]. Not Sir John ? [*Consults watch.*] It's only half-past three.

EUSTACE. No—only little Glaisher. He said he was too early. However, as *you* weren't there he came and had a look at *me*.

MRS. JACKSON. What did he say, dear ?

EUSTACE. Said I was getting on all right. He's coming to have another look at me in a day or two.

MR. JACKSON. When does he think you'll be well enough to get to work again ?

EUSTACE. I don't know. I didn't ask him.

MRS. JACKSON. Oh, Samuel, it's too soon to think of that *yet !* The poor boy's only convalescent. Wait till Dr. Glaisher has stopped his visits.

[HENRY *snorts.*]

EUSTACE. My dear Henry, what extraordinary noises you make. It's a terrible habit. You should see some one about it. Why not consult Glaisher ?

MR. JACKSON [*to his wife*]. As you please, dear. Still, I *should* like to know what Eustace intends to do when he *is* well enough. I'm bound to say he *looks* perfectly well.

EUSTACE [*blandly*]. Appearances are so deceptive, father.

[VIOLET *comes out of house and goes up to her mother. She has some work in her hands.*]

VIOLET. Got back, mother dear ? [*Kisses her.*] Enjoyed your lunch ?

MRS. JACKSON. Very much. It was quite a large party.

VIOLET [*sitting down*]. What did you talk about?

MRS. JACKSON. About your father's election principally. They say Parliament may dissolve any day now. What are you making, dear?

VIOLET. Handkerchiefs. I promised Eustace I'd work some initials for him.

MR. JACKSON [*returning doggedly to his subject*]. Perhaps you will be good enough to tell me what your plans are, Eustace.

EUSTACE. I haven't any plans, father.

MR. JACKSON. You haven't any?

MRS. JACKSON. Eustace said the other day he thought he would like to be a doctor.

MR. JACKSON. A doctor! Nonsense.

MRS. JACKSON [*mildly*]. Well, I only tell you what he said.

EUSTACE [*blandly*]. My remark was not intended to be taken literally. I don't seriously propose to enter the medical profession.

MR. JACKSON [*irritably*]. Do you seriously propose anything?

EUSTACE. No, father. I don't know that I do.

MR. JACKSON [*meditatively*]. I might perhaps find you a place in the office.

HENRY [*firmly*]. No, father! *I* object to that.

VIOLET. Henry!

HENRY. Yes, I do. I object to the office being used as a dumping-ground for incompetents.

MRS. JACKSON [*protesting*]. Henry! Your own brother!

HENRY. I can't help that. I don't see why the firm should be expected to pay a salary to someone who is utterly useless merely because he's my brother.

MR. JACKSON. Still, we might *try* him.

HENRY. My dear father, why not face the truth ? You know what Eustace is. We got him into Jenkins' office. He made nothing of it. Then he was in the Gloucester and Wiltshire Bank. No use there. He tried farming. Same result. Finally you gave him a thousand pounds to settle in Australia. That was five years ago, and here he is back again without a sixpence.

MRS. JACKSON. Eustace has been very unlucky.

HENRY [*impatiently*]. What has *luck* got to do with it ? Eustace doesn't *work*. That's what's the matter with *him*.

MRS. JACKSON. Still, if he had another chance——

HENRY. My dear mother, you always believe people ought to have another chance. It's a little mania with you. Eustace has had dozens of chances. He's made a mess of every one of them. You know that as well as I do.

MR. JACKSON. Yes. There's no use hiding it from ourselves.

HENRY. Not the least—as we can't hide it from any one else.

MR. JACKSON [*after a pause*]. Well, Eustace, what do *you* think ?

EUSTACE [*airily*]. I ? Oh, I agree with Henry.
                    [*Lights another cigarette.*

MR. JACKSON. You *what ?*

EUSTACE. I agree with Henry. I think he's

diagnosed the case with great accuracy. Henry ought to have been a doctor, too!

MR. JACKSON [*getting up angrily and making an oration*]. Now look here, Eustace. I've had enough of this. You seem to imagine because you've been ill, and come home in rags, nothing more in the way of work is to be expected of you. You're to loll about in a hammock smoking cigarettes, and taking not the smallest interest in any plans that are suggested for your future. Henry says the reason you've always been a failure is that you don't work, and you say you agree with him. Very well. What I have to tell you is I'm not going to have you loafing away your time here. I disapprove of loafing on principle. Both as a public man and as a private man I disapprove of it. There's far too much of it in England to-day. That's where the Germans are ahead of us. Young men who ought to be at business or in the professions idle away their time and live on their parents. That won't do for *me*. I insist upon your getting something to do at once and doing it. I insist upon it. If you don't——

[*During the last sentence of this impassioned oration, SIR JOHN and LADY FARINGFORD and STELLA come out of the house, preceded by BAINES.*]

BAINES. Sir John and Lady Faringford, Miss Faringford.

[*Instant change of front on the part of the whole family. MR. JACKSON, who has been haranguing his son almost as though he were at a public meeting,*] *stops short in the midst of his peroration, and hurriedly substitutes a glassy smile for the irascible sternness which marked his features a moment before.* MRS. JACKSON *and the others, who had listened in uncomfortable silence to* MR. JACKSON's *eloquence, hastily assume the conventional simper of politeness as they rise to receive their guests. The only person who remains quite self-possessed is* EUSTACE, *who smiles sardonically as he gets out of his hammock.*]

EUSTACE [*aside to* HENRY]. Poor old governor ! Stemmed in full tide !

MRS. JACKSON. Dear Lady Faringford. How nice of you to come ! Stella, my dear.

[*Shakes hands with them and with* SIR JOHN.

LADY FARINGFORD. As Sir John was due at your husband's Committee at four, Stella and I thought we would drive him down.

MRS. JACKSON. You'll stay and have some tea now you are here, of course ?

LADY FARINGFORD. Thank you. Tea would be very pleasant.

STELLA [*shaking hands with* HENRY]. How do you do ? And how is the invalid ? [*Throwing a bright smile to* EUSTACE.] Getting on well ?

HENRY [*grimly*]. Excellently.

STELLA. That's right.

[*Shakes hands with* EUSTACE. *To* HENRY]

He really looks better, doesn't he ? Dr. Glaisher says it's been a wonderful recovery.

HENRY. I suppose he does !

STELLA [*to* MR. JACKSON.] How glad you must be to have him home again.

ACT III   179

MR. JACKSON [*with ghastly attempt at effusion*]. It's a great pleasure, of course.

STELLA.   It must be so sad for parents when their children go away from them.   But I suppose sons *will* go away sometimes, however hard their parents try to keep them.   Won't they ?

MR. JACKSON.   That does happen sometimes—er —unquestionably. [*More briskly.*]   And, anyhow, young men can't stay at home always, my dear Miss Faringford.   They have their own way to make in the world.

STELLA.   And so the parents *have* to let them go. It seems hard.   But when they come back it must be delightful.

EUSTACE. *It is.*

[*During the following scene* HENRY *makes one or two unsuccessful efforts to approach* STELLA, *but* EUSTACE *blandly outmanœuvres him, and secures her for himself. They chat together in the friendliest fashion, while* HENRY *fumes inwardly.*]

SIR JOHN.   Hadn't we better be going in, Jackson ?   I sha'n't be able to stay very long.   I have to meet my agent at 5.15 sharp to see about some fences.

MR. JACKSON [*looks at watch*].   It's barely four yet.   We'd better wait a minute or two.   Glaisher will arrive directly, and then we can get to work.

SIR JOHN.   Ling's advertised to speak at Maytree, I see, to-morrow week.

MR. JACKSON.   Is he ?   At Maytree ?   That's rather out of his country.

SIR JOHN.   Yes.   He doesn't go down so well in

the villages. Thank heaven agriculture is still conservative. They go to his meetings, though.

STELLA [*throwing a remark to* MR. JACKSON]. Mr. Ling is such a good speaker, they say.

EUSTACE. My father is a good speaker, too, when he's roused, Miss Faringford. You should have heard him ten minutes ago.

SIR JOHN. What was he speaking on?

EUSTACE [*airily*]. The Unemployed.

[MR. JACKSON *nearly explodes at this, but, remembering that visitors are present, controls himself by a great effort.*]

SIR JOHN. I congratulate you, Jackson. It isn't all sons who are so appreciative of their father's efforts. *My* son never listens to *me !*

[MR. JACKSON *smiles wanly.*]

[*Enter* BAINES *announcing* DR. GLAISHER *and exit.*]

[DR. GLAISHER *issues from house, and steps briskly on to the lawn, with a resolute pretence that time is money to him—although he knows it isn't.*]

MR. JACKSON. Ah, here you are, Doctor. I began to think you weren't coming.

MRS. JACKSON [*shaking hands*]. Good afternoon. Why didn't you bring Mrs. Glaisher? She and I and Lady Faringford could have entertained each other while you were all at your Committee.

DR. GLAISHER. She would have enjoyed it of all things. But I left her at home with the children. Tommy has the whooping-cough just now, and requires a lot of nursing.

MRS. JACKSON. Poor little chap. I hope he'll
be better soon.

MR. JACKSON [*looking at watch*]. Well, well, I'm
afraid we ought to go in. Come, Sir John. Are
you ready, Doctor ? Shall I lead the way ? Come,
Henry.   [*Fusses off importantly.*

SIR JOHN. By all means.

MRS. JACKSON [*calling after him*]. As you are
going would you mind ringing the bell, Samuel, and
telling Baines to bring tea out here ?

MR. JACKSON. Very well, my dear.

[MR. JACKSON, SIR JOHN, THE DOCTOR, *and* HENRY
go off into the house to their Committee. MRS.
JACKSON, LADY FARINGFORD, *and* VIOLET *seat themselves by the table, to which tea is presently brought
by* BAINES *and the* FOOTMAN. STELLA *selects a chair
rather further off, where she is soon joined by* EUSTACE.]

LADY FARINGFORD. I do hope your husband will
be elected, Mrs. Jackson. Mr. Ling has the most
dreadful opinions about land—and, indeed, about
everything else, I'm told. But that is of less
importance.

MRS. JACKSON. Indeed ?

LADY FARINGFORD. Oh yes. Only a year ago,
at a meeting of the Parish Council, he made a speech
attacking Sir John quite violently about one of his
cottages. It was let to young Barrett, quite a
respectable, hard-working man—who afterwards
died of pneumonia. Mr. Ling declared the cottage
was damp, and not fit for any one to live in. So
ridiculous of him ! As if *all* cottages were not
damp. The absurd part of it was that afterwards,

when Mrs. Barrett was left a widow and Sir John gave her notice because she couldn't pay her rent, and he wanted to convert the cottage into pigsties, Mr. Ling was equally indignant, and seemed to think we ought to find Mrs. Barrett another house! I don't think he can be quite right in his head.

VIOLET. Shall I make the tea, mother?

MRS. JACKSON. If you please, dear.

[VIOLET *gives her mother and* LADY FARINGFORD *their tea.* EUSTACE *takes a cup to* STELLA.]

EUSTACE. What do *you* think about damp cottages, Miss Faringford? Do you think they ought to be left standing in order that the labourer may live in them—and have pneumonia. Or be pulled down in order that the labourer may have nowhere to live at all?

STELLA. I don't know. I think it's dreadful there should be damp cottages anywhere.

EUSTACE. That would never do. There must be good cottages and bad cottages, in order that the strong may get the good cottages and the weak the bad.

STELLA. You mean in order that the strong may have the bad cottages and the weak the good. They need them more.

EUSTACE. That would be quite unscientific. No, the strong must have the good cottages in order that they may grow stronger. And the weak must have the bad cottages in order that they may die off. Survival of the fittest, you know.

STELLA. How horrible!

EUSTACE. Yes, but how necessary !

LADY FARINGFORD [*noticing that* EUSTACE *has drawn up a chair and seated himself by her daughter*]. Come over here, Stella. You have the sun on your face there.

STELLA [*rising unwillingly*]. Very well, mamma. [*Moves to a chair on the other side of the tea table less unfortunately situated.*]

LADY FARINGFORD. By the way, Mrs. Jackson, have you heard about poor Miss Higgs, who used to keep the school at Little Chedleigh and play the harmonium so badly on Sundays ? You remember her ? Quite a good creature, knew all kinds of subjects, and never expected one to take any notice of her. So, of course, one never did. Well, two years ago an aunt died and left her a little money, and Miss Higgs retired and went to live in Gloucester. One of those unattractive houses near the canal. But she seems to have been quite incapable of managing money. Put it into a gold-mine, I believe, or gave it to her solicitor to invest— which comes to the same thing—and lost every penny.

MRS. JACKSON. Oh ! *Poor* Miss Higgs. What a sad thing.

LADY FARINGFORD. Fortunately, she was so affected by her loss that she drowned herself in the canal at the bottom of her garden. Otherwise I'm afraid some sort of a subscription would have had to be got up for her.

[EUSTACE *gets another cup of tea from* VIOLET, *and takes advantage of the move to sit down by* STELLA *again.* LADY FARINGFORD *notices this manœuvre with hardly concealed irritation, and, from this point till she rises to go, watches* EUSTACE'S *attentions to her daughter resentfully out of the corner of her eye.*]

VIOLET. I liked Miss Higgs very much, Lady Faringford.

LADY FARINGFORD. So did quite a number of people, I'm told. She was quite a good creature, as I said, much superior to the young woman who has succeeded her at Little Chedleigh. I wanted them to give the place to my maid Dawkins, who is getting rather past her work, and really could have taught everything that is necessary or wholesome for the lower orders to learn, though I dare say she might have had some difficulty with the harmonium—at first. However, they preferred to get down a young person from London with the most elaborate qualifications. So highly educated, in fact, that I hear she can't *teach* at all.

MRS. JACKSON. How very awkward.

LADY FARINGFORD. It is indeed.

[*Swift glance towards* EUSTACE *and her daughter, who are obviously far too much interested in one another*] Stella !

STELLA. Yes, mamma.

LADY FARINGFORD. Say good-bye to Mrs. Jackson, my dear. We really must be going. [*Rising.*

MRS. JACKSON [*rising also*]. Shall I let Sir John know you are ready ?

LADY FARINGFORD. Pray don't trouble. We can pick him up as we go through the house. Good-bye, Mrs. Jackson. [*To* EUSTACE, *shaking hands.*]

Good-bye. When do you go back to Australia? *Quite* soon, I hope. Come, Stella.

STELLA [*shaking hands*]. Good-bye, Mr. Jackson.

[LADY FARINGFORD *and* STELLA *take their departure through the French windows, accompanied by* VIOLET. *Their tea has been sadly curtailed, and so has the meeting of* SIR JOHN'S *Committee, but* LADY FARINGFORD *feels that no sacrifices are too great to nip an incipient flirtation between her daughter and* EUSTACE. *As soon as they have gone,* EUSTACE *goes and sits by his mother.*]

EUSTACE. Clever woman, that.

MRS. JACKSON. Is she, dear? I hadn't noticed.

EUSTACE. Yes. We're all of us selfish. But most of us make an effort to conceal the fact. With the result that we are always being asked to do something for somebody and having to invent elaborate excuses for not doing it. And that makes us very unpopular. For every one hates asking for anything —unless he gets it. But Lady Faringford proclaims her selfishness so openly that no one ever dreams of asking her to do things. It would be tempting Providence. With the result that I expect she's quite a popular woman.

MRS. JACKSON. I'm glad you like Lady Faringford, dear. Your father has the highest opinion of her.

EUSTACE. Yes. The governor never could see an inch before his nose.

MRS. JACKSON. Can't he, dear? He has never said anything about it.

Eustace [*patting her hand affectionately*]. Dear mother !

[Violet *returns.*]

Seen the Gorgon safely off the premises ?

Violet [*laughing*]. Yes—and Sir John.

Mrs. Jackson. The Committee was over, then ?

Violet. It is now—as Lady Faringford insisted on carrying off the chairman. Here is father.

[Mr. Jackson *and* Henry *come out of house.* Baines *follows hard after them, with letters on salver. He hands three of these to* Mr. Jackson, *two to* Mrs. Jackson, *and one to* Violet.]

Baines. Shall I take away, madam ?

Mrs. Jackson. Wait a moment. [*To* Mr. Jackson.] Will you have any tea, Samuel ?

Mr. Jackson [*opening long envelope and reading contents*]. No. We had some indoors.

Mrs. Jackson [*to* Baines]. Yes, you can take away. [*To* Mr. Jackson.] Did you have a successful meeting ?

[Baines *beckons to* Footman, *who comes out, and together they take away tea.*]

Mr. Jackson [*standing by table, still reading*]. Eh ? Oh yes.

Mrs. Jackson [*to* Henry]. What a pity Sir John had to go.

Henry. It didn't matter. We'd pretty nearly got through our business.

[Mrs. Jackson *opens her letter, and becomes absorbed in its contents.*]

ACT III   187

MR. JACKSON [*handing papers to* HENRY]. You'd better look through these. They're from Fisher and Thompson. It's about Wenhams' mill. The sale is next week.

HENRY [*nods*]. Very well.

MR. JACKSON [*taking a seat at the table, and clearing his throat with dignity*]. Now, Eustace, I want to have a serious talk with you.

EUSTACE. Not *again*, father.

MR. JACKSON [*puzzled*]. What do you mean?

EUSTACE. Couldn't you put it off till to-morrow? I'm hardly well enough to talk seriously twice in one day.

MR. JACKSON. Nonsense, sir. You're perfectly well. Glaisher says there's no longer the slightest cause for anxiety.

EUSTACE. The traitor!

MR. JACKSON. What, sir?

EUSTACE. Nothing, father.

MR. JACKSON. As I told you before tea, I'm not going to have you idling away your time here. The question is, what are we to do?

EUSTACE. Just so, father.

MR. JACKSON. I mean, what are *you* to do?

[*Pause. No remark from* EUSTACE.]

Lady Faringford said as she went away you ought to go back to Australia. She said it was a thousand pities for any young man *not* to go to Australia.

MRS. JACKSON. Eustace was just saying how clever Lady Faringford was when you came out.

MR. JACKSON. I'm glad to hear it. [*To* EUSTACE.] Well, what do you think?

EUSTACE. About Australia ?

MR. JACKSON. Yes.

EUSTACE. I don't think anything about it.

MR. JACKSON. Would you like to go out there again ?

EUSTACE. No, I shouldn't. I've been there once. It was an utter failure.

MR. JACKSON. *You* were a failure, you mean.

EUSTACE. As you please. Anyway, it was no good, and I had to work as a navvy on the railway. I don't propose to do that again.

HENRY [*looking up from* FISHER *and* THOMPSON'S *papers*]. Other people do well in Australia.

EUSTACE. Other people do well in England. Or rather, the same people do well in both.

MR. JACKSON [*peevishly*]. What *do* you mean ?

EUSTACE. Simply that the kind of qualities which make for success in one country make for success in another. It's just as easy to fail in Sydney as in London. I've done it and I know.

MRS. JACKSON [*who has just opened her second letter*]. A letter from Janet. She's going to be at Gloucester next week, and would like to come over and see us on Friday. We aren't going out on that day, are we, Vi ?

[MR. JACKSON, *impatient at this interruption, opens the second of his letters and glances at it.*]

VIOLET. No, mother.

MRS. JACKSON. That will do, then. She'd better come to luncheon. [*Rises.*] I'll write and tell her at once before I forget.

VIOLET. Shall I do it, mother ?

MRS. JACKSON. No, dear. I can manage it.

[*Goes into house.*

MR. JACKSON [*who has opened his third letter, and contemplated its contents with indignant amazement, strikes the table with his open hand*]. Well!

VIOLET. What is it, father?

MR. JACKSON. What's the meaning of this, I wonder! Barton must be out of his senses.

VIOLET. Barton?

MR. JACKSON. Yes, Barton. The tailor. Why does he send me in a bill like this? Twenty-five pounds! And I've had nothing from him since Easter. Listen to this. One lounge suit four guineas, one dress suit eight guineas, one flannel suit three pounds ten, another lounge suit four guineas, one frock coat and waistcoat four guineas, one pair of trousers one guinea. Total, twenty-five pounds eleven.

EUSTACE [*whose energies are absorbed at the moment in blowing through a cigarette-holder*]. They're mine, father.

MR. JACKSON. What, sir!

EUSTACE [*calmly*]. Some clothes I ordered. I told him to send the bill to you. That's all right, isn't it?

MR. JACKSON [*exploding*]. All right! Certainly not, sir. It's very far from right. It's a great liberty.

EUSTACE. My dear father, the bill must be sent in to somebody.

MR. JACKSON. And why not to you, pray?

EUSTACE. What would be the good of that, father. I've nothing to pay it with.

MR. JACKSON. Then you shouldn't have ordered the things.

EUSTACE. But I must wear something. I can't go on wearing Henry's things indefinitely. It's hard on *him !*

[HENRY *snorts.*]

My dear Henry !

MR. JACKSON [*gobbling with indignation*]. But what's become of all the clothes you had ? You must have had *some* clothes.

EUSTACE [*shrugs*]. They're in London—and in rags.

MR. JACKSON. Now look here, Eustace. I'm not going to have this. I'm not going to have a son of mine running up bills here.

EUSTACE. All right, father. I'm quite willing to pay for the things—if you give me the money.

MR. JACKSON. I shall *not* give you the money, sir. If you want money you must earn it.

EUSTACE. That doesn't take us very far.

[*At this* MR. JACKSON *rises and invokes the heavens.*]

MR. JACKSON. You'll disgrace me. That's what will happen. I insist on your paying Barton, and giving me your word of honour never to get anything on credit here again.

[*Thrusts bill into* EUSTACE's *hand and tramps about angrily.*]

EUSTACE. I've no objection. I don't run up tailors' bills for pleasure. I'd just as soon pay ready money as you would. Only I haven't got it. Give me twenty pounds—no, twenty-five pounds eleven —and I'll pay Barton to-morrow.

Mr. Jackson. I decline to give you money. I decline. Your request is impudent.

Eustace [*blandly*]. Let's keep our tempers, father.

Mr. Jackson. *What*, sir ?

Eustace. I merely suggested we should keep our tempers. That's all.

Mr. Jackson. This is intolerable. I disown you, sir. I disown you.

Violet. Father !

Mr. Jackson. Be silent, Violet. [*To* Eustace.] I'll have nothing more to do with you. I'll pay this debt to Barton—and any others you may have incurred since you came back. After that I've done with you. Leave my house at once.

Eustace [*rising, and throwing away his cigarette. He has his temper admirably under control, but speaks with ominous distinctness*]. Very well, father. I'll go if you wish it. But I warn you if I do go it will be to the nearest workhouse !

Mr. Jackson [*fuming*]. That's your affair. It has nothing to do with me.   [*Turns away.*

Eustace. I question that. It rather knocks your election prospects on the head, I fancy.

Mr. Jackson [*swinging round*]. Eh ? What ?

Eustace. You don't seriously suppose if I do this you'll be returned for Parliament ? If you do you don't know the British Electorate. This is going to be a scandal, a scandal worth five hundred votes to the other side. And the last man's majority was only fifty. Oh no, my dear father, if it comes out that the son of the rich Conservative candidate is in the local workhouse, good-bye to your chances in *this* constituency.

HENRY. You wouldn't dare!

EUSTACE. Dare? Nonsense. What have I to lose?

HENRY. But this is infamous. It's blackmail.

EUSTACE [*contemptuously*]. Call it what you like. It's what I propose to do if you force me to it.

VIOLET. Eustace! You couldn't be so wicked!

EUSTACE [*more gently*]. My dear Vi, have I any choice? Here am I absolutely penniless. The governor flies into a rage because I order some clothes from his tailor, and turns me into the street. What am I to do? I've no profession, no business I can turn my hand to. I might take to manual labour, I suppose, break stones on the road. But that would bring equal discredit on this highly respectable family. In England sons of wealthy cloth manufacturers don't work with their hands. Besides, I don't like work. So there's nothing left but to beg. If I beg in the street the police will take me up. Therefore I must beg from my relations. If they refuse me I must go on the Parish.

HENRY. Father, this is monstrous. I wouldn't submit to it if I were you. If he wants to prevent your election let him. I advise you to refuse.

EUSTACE. All right. But it knocks *your* prospects on the head, too, my dear Henry—social advancement and love's young dream, you know. Miss Faringford won't marry you if this happens. Her mother won't let her. You're not so rich as all that. And if her mother would, Stella wouldn't.

Stella rather likes me. In fact, I think she likes me better than she does you at present. I'm not absolutely certain she wouldn't marry me if I asked her.

HENRY. Lady Faringford would forbid her.

EUSTACE. Perhaps we shouldn't consult her. Anyhow, if you leave me to eat skilly in Chedleigh Workhouse, Stella won't accept you. I lay you ten to one on it.

[HENRY *opens his mouth to speak, realises that he has nothing to say, and shuts it again. All silent. Then a gong rings loudly inside the house. Another pause.*]

Well, father, what do you say ?

[*Another silence.* MR. JACKSON, *nonplussed, turns away.*]

Nothing ? *You*, Henry. *You're* full of resource ! What do *you* think ?

[*But* HENRY *apparently is equally at a loss, for he says nothing. Another pause.* EUSTACE *shrugs his shoulders.*]

Well, first gong's gone. *I* shall go and dress for dinner.

[*Lounges off into the house as the curtain falls.*

ACT IV

SCENE.—*The drawing-room at Chedleigh as we saw it in the first Act. Some three hours have elapsed since* EUSTACE *exploded his bomb-shell. When the curtain rises,* MRS. JACKSON *is sitting in an easy chair, nodding over a piece of work of some kind.* VIOLET *is at the piano, playing softly. Presently* EUSTACE *wanders in.* VIOLET *stops playing, closes piano, and comes down towards fireplace, later taking up handkerchief she is working for* EUSTACE.

MRS. JACKSON [*waking up, drowsily*]. Is that you, Eustace ? Where's your father ?

EUSTACE [*going to her*]. In the library with Henry.

MRS. JACKSON. Talking business ?

EUSTACE [*nods*]. Yes.

MRS. JACKSON. Can you see the time, Vi ?

VIOLET [*sitting by fireplace*]. Nearly ten, mother dear.

MRS. JACKSON. So late ! They must be discussing something very important.

EUSTACE [*grimly*]. They are.

MRS. JACKSON. Have they been long in the library ?

EUSTACE. They went directly you and Vi left the table.

MRS. JACKSON. And you've been alone in the

dining-room all that time ? Why didn't you come in to us ?

EUSTACE. I thought they might want to consult me.

MRS. JACKSON [*beaming*]. About business ? I'm so glad. I'm sure you would be most useful in the business if you tried, though Henry doesn't think so.

EUSTACE. Are you, mother ?

MRS. JACKSON. Of course. Why not ? Henry is. And you always learnt your lessons far quicker than Henry when you were a boy.

EUSTACE [*laying hand on her shoulder*]. Flatterer !

MRS. JACKSON [*putting work into work-basket*]. Well, I don't think I'll stay up any longer. [*Rises.*] And I do hope Henry won't keep your father up late. It can't be good for him. [*Kisses* EUSTACE.] Goodnight, dear. Sleep well. Are you coming, Vi ?

[*Kisses her.*

VIOLET. Directly, mother.

[EUSTACE *holds open door for his mother to go out. Then comes slowly down and sits in chair by* VIOLET.]

EUSTACE. Dear old mater. She's not clever, but for real goodness of heart I don't know her equal.

VIOLET [*impatiently*]. Clever ! I'm sick of cleverness. What's the good of it ? You're *clever*. What has it done for you ?

EUSTACE. Kept me out of prison. That's always something.

[VIOLET *makes gesture of protest.*]

Oh yes, it has. There have been times when I was so hard up I felt I would do anything, *anything*, just for a square meal. If I had been a stupid man I should have done it. I should have robbed a till or forged a cheque, and that would have been the end of me. Fortunately, I'd brains enough to realise that that kind of thing always gets found out. So here I am, still a blameless member of society.

[VIOLET *says nothing, but goes on working steadily.* Pause.]

The mater hasn't been told?

VIOLET. About what happened before dinner? No.

EUSTACE. I'm glad of that.

VIOLET. Why?

EUSTACE [*impatiently*]. My dear Vi, I'm not absolutely inhuman. Because I'm fond of her, of course, and don't like giving her pain.

VIOLET. She'll have to know sooner or later.

EUSTACE. Then I'd rather it was later; in fact, when I'm not here. If anybody has got to suffer on my account I'd rather not see it.

VIOLET. And you call Lady Faringford selfish!

EUSTACE [*carelessly*]. Yes. It's a quality I particularly dislike—in others.

VIOLET [*stopping her work for a moment and looking at him wonderingly*]. I can't understand you. As a boy you were so different. You were kind and affectionate and thoughtful for others.

EUSTACE [*shrugs*]. I dare say.

VIOLET. And now——! [*Earnestly.*] Think

what you have made of your life! You had good
abilities. You might have done almost anything
if you had only tried. You might have been a
successful, honourable man, with an assured position
and a record you could be proud of. You might——

EUSTACE [*putting his fingers in his ears*]. Stop,
Vi; stop, I tell you. I won't listen to you.

VIOLET [*surprised*]. Why not?

EUSTACE [*doggedly*]. Because I won't. All that
is over. What's past is past. I have to live my
life *now*. Do you suppose it would make it any
easier for me to grizzle over wasted opportunities?
No! As each year passes I turn over the page and
forget it.

VIOLET [*wondering*]. And do you never look
back?

EUSTACE [*with a slight shiver*]. Never! If I did
I should have drowned myself long ago.

VIOLET [*with horror*]. Eustace!

EUSTACE [*exasperated*]. Oh, my dear Vi, it's all
very well for you to preach, but you don't understand. It's easy enough for you living comfortably
here at home, working for your bazaars and visiting
your old women. Your life slips away in a quiet
round of small duties, paying calls with the mater,
pouring out the governor's coffee. One day just
like another. You've no anxieties, no temptations.
The lines have fallen to you in pleasant places. And
you think you can sit in judgment on me!

VIOLET [*quietly, resuming her work*]. You think
my life happier than yours, then?

EUSTACE. Isn't it?

VIOLET [*shaking her head*]. No. *Your* life is your

own. You can do as you please with it, use it or waste it as you think best. You are free. I am not. You think because I stay quietly at home, doing the duty that lies nearest me and not crying out against fate, therefore I've nothing more to wish for. Would *you* be happy, do you suppose, if you were in my case ? I live here down in Chedleigh from year's end to year's end. Mother never leaves home. She doesn't care to pay visits. So I cannot either. I may sometimes get away for a few days, a week, perhaps, but very seldom. And as mother grows older I shall go less. Soon people will give up asking me when they find I always refuse. And so I shall be left here alone with no friends, no real companionship, merely one of the family obliged to know the people they know, visit the people they visit, not a grown woman with interests of her own and a life to order as she pleases.

EUSTACE. But you'll marry ?

VIOLET. Marry ! What chance have I of marrying now ? When we hadn't so much money, and Henry and father weren't so set on taking a position in the county, there was some chance for me. Now there is none. It's all very well for Henry. He is a partner in the firm. He will be a very rich man. He can marry Stella Faringford. Oh, we are to be great people ! But you don't find Sir John Faringford's son proposing to *me !* No ! He wants a girl of his own class or else an heiress, not a manufacturer's daughter with a few thousand pounds. So the great people won't marry me and I mustn't marry the little people. Father wouldn't like it. He hardly lets mother ask them to the house nowadays.

And so the years go by and my youth with them, and I know it will be like this always, always.

EUSTACE. Poor old Vi! And I thought you were quite contented with your bazaars and your old women. Why don't you speak to the mater?

VIOLET [*with a shrug that is half a sigh*]. What's the use? Mother wouldn't understand. She married when she was twenty-one. She doesn't know what it is for a girl to go on living at home long after she's grown up and ought to have a house of her own. So I stay on here knitting socks for old Allen and working *your* handkerchiefs, and here I shall stay till mother and father are both dead. . . . And then it will be too late.

EUSTACE. Poor old Vi! . . . [*A pause.*] Do you know, you make me feel rather mean? Henry and the governor I can stand up to. They're very much like me. We belong to the predatory type. Only they're more successful than I am. They live on their workpeople. I propose to live on them. We're birds of a feather. But you're different. I suppose you get it from the mater.

VIOLET. Why are you so bitter against your father?

EUSTACE. Am I?

VIOLET. Yes. Just now. And this afternoon.

EUSTACE [*shrugs*]. Oh, that—! Well, the fact is, I wanted to bring things to a head. I feel I can't stay here. I must get away.

VIOLET. Why?

EUSTACE. For lots of reasons. I can't stand this place. I've outgrown it, I suppose. [*Pause.*] And then there's Stella——

VIOLET. Stella ?

EUSTACE. Yes. If I were here much longer I might be falling in love with Stella. And that wouldn't be fair to Henry. After all, he was first in the field. And it wouldn't be fair to her either. I'm not fit to marry a girl like that. No. I must get away.

VIOLET [*touched*]. Poor Eustace.

EUSTACE. Oh, you needn't *pity* me. I shall get along somehow. My life hasn't been successful. It hasn't even been honourable. But it's been devilish interesting.

[*The door opens, and* MR. JACKSON *and* HENRY *enter.* MR. JACKSON *passes* EUSTACE *in dignified silence, and turns to his daughter.*]

MR. JACKSON. You here, Vi ? I thought you'd have gone to bed. Your mother went long ago, I expect ?

VIOLET. Only a few minutes.

MR. JACKSON. Well, run away now, dear. It's late.

VIOLET. Very well, · father. [*Gathers up her things and rises.*] Good-night. [*Kisses him.*] Good-night, Henry. Good-night, Eustace.

EUSTACE [*taking her hand*]. Good-night, Vi. And good-bye.

[*He goes to the door and opens it for her. She kisses him and goes out. He closes the door after her and slowly turns back to the others, to find* MR. JACKSON *in a commanding position on the hearthrug, and* HENRY *standing by the piano. * EUSTACE *selects a settee at the opposite side of the room from his father, makes himself comfortable on it, and waits for one of the others to speak. Neither does so, however, and after a minute or more has elapsed, * EUSTACE, *feeling the silence to be rather grotesque, breaks it.*]

EUSTACE [*cheerfully*]. Well ?

MR. JACKSON [*coughs nervously, then plunges into his subject*]. Ahem ! We have been in consultation, your brother and I, as to the right course to adopt with regard to you.

EUSTACE [*nods*]. So I supposed.

[HENRY *finds a chair about equidistant from his father and his brother, and sits down.*]

MR. JACKSON [*with great dignity*]. After the extraordinary and—er—undutiful attitude you took up this afternoon, I might naturally have declined all further relations with you. But——

EUSTACE [*matter of fact*]. But as that course might prove almost as disagreeable for yourself as it would for me, you naturally thought better of it. Let's get on.

MR. JACKSON [*rearing under this touch of the spur, but mastering himself*]. I might point out to you that we, your mother and I, have never failed in our duty by you. We have been indulgent parents. You were sent to a first-rate school. Nothing was spared that could make you a prosperous and success-ful man. But I won't speak of that.

EUSTACE [*dryly*]. Thanks, father.

MR. JACKSON [*running on*]. I might point out

that we have given you a score of good chances for establishing yourself in a satisfactory position, and you have failed to profit by them. I might remind you that since you returned to this roof——

EUSTACE [*impatiently*]. My dear father, I thought you were going to leave that part out ? And I do wish you wouldn't begin talking about your *roof*. When people refer to their *roof* I always know they're going to suggest something quite unpractical. In ordinary times they don't soar above the ceiling. But in moments of fervour off goes the roof ! Let's come to the point.

MR. JACKSON [*rearing again, but again controlling himself*]. I will do so at once. . . . Your brother and I feel that little as you have deserved this consideration at my hands, and wholly as you have forfeited all claim to further assistance both by your past failures and by your conduct this afternoon, you should yet be given one more chance.

[EUSTACE *insensibly begins to beat time to his father's impassioned antitheses.*]

EUSTACE. Come, that's satisfactory.

MR. JACKSON. Five years ago when, after repeated failures on your part, after paying your debts more than once and finding you openings again and again, I sent you to Australia. I gave you a thousand pounds to make a career for yourself. I told you that was the last sum of money you would have from me during my lifetime. What may—or may not— come to you after my death is another matter. And I gave it you on the express stipulation that if you lost or squandered it you were not to write for more.

EUSTACE. I kept that stipulation.

MR. JACKSON. That is so. I now propose to do again what I did five years ago. I propose to send you back to Australia with a thousand pounds.

HENRY [*looking up from book which he has been appearing to read*]. To be paid to you *after* your arrival there.

MR. JACKSON. Exactly. I will send the thousand pounds, less the cost of your passage, to an agent, to be paid to you on your landing. In return for this you are to promise not to come back to this country without my express permission.

[MR. JACKSON *pauses for a suitable expression of gratitude from his son. None, however, is forthcoming, and he has to go on without it.*]

I think you will agree with me that the course I am taking is a kinder one than you deserve. Few fathers would do as much. I might have named a smaller sum. But I prefer to err on the generous side.

EUSTACE [*nodding*]. Quite so. [*With genuine curiosity.*] And what do you propose that I should do with a thousand pounds ?

MR. JACKSON. That is for you to decide. You might start in business.

EUSTACE. I've tried that.

MR. JACKSON. Sheep farming.

EUSTACE. I've tried that.

MR. JACKSON. Gold mining.

EUSTACE. I've tried that.

MR. JACKSON [*annoyed*]. Well, well, any line which you think offers you a favourable opening.

EUSTACE [*insinuatingly*]. And which line is that ?

MR. JACKSON [*irritably*]. I don't know.

EUSTACE. No more do I. [*Pause.*] No, father, it would be absurd for me to accept your offer, because it isn't practical. It would only be throwing your money away. It would do me no good, and cause you heartfelt distress.

MR. JACKSON. Nonsense. Other young fellows go out to Australia with less than a thousand pounds and make *fortunes !* Far less ! Why shouldn't you ?

EUSTACE. Why, indeed ? However, we must keep to the point. *They* make fortunes. *I* don't.

MR. JACKSON [*exasperated*]. In fact, they're active and energetic, you're useless and worthless. Where other people by thrift and enterprise and steady application *make* money, you only *lose* it.

EUSTACE. Exactly. I lose it. And doubtless for lack of the qualities you mention. What then ? Granted I am all you say, how does that help us ? Here I am, alive, and requiring food at the customary intervals. Who is going to give it me ?

[HENRY *snorts.*]

Really, Henry !

MR. JACKSON [*hotly*]. That is to say you *want* to go through life sponging on your family instead of working for your living like an honest man !

EUSTACE [*very nearly losing his temper at what seems to him the amazing stupidity of this remark*]. Look here, father, hadn't we better drop all that stuff about *wanting* to sponge on one's family and the rest of it ? Nobody *wants* to sponge on other people. The idea's preposterous. We all *want* to be prosperous and highly respected members of Society like you and Henry, with more money than we know what to do with, with a seat in Parliament and a wife out of the Baronetage. That's what we *want*. And if we haven't the luck or the brains or the energy to get it, you needn't call us names. You don't suppose I *prefer* losing money to making it, do you ? You don't suppose if I had my *choice* I should drift about the world adding up accounts in a filthy Hong-kong bank or playing steward on a filthier ocean liner ? You can't be so ridiculous. I'm good for nothing, as you say. I've no push, no initiative, no staying power. I shall never be anything but a failure. But don't imagine I *like* it ! You seem to think you've a terrible grievance because I'm a ne'er-do-well and come to you for money, but the real grievance is mine.

HENRY. If you don't like coming on your family for money, you needn't do it.

EUSTACE [*impatiently*]. It's not what I do but what I am that is the difficulty. What does it matter what one *does?* It's done, and then it's over and one can forget it. The real tragedy is what one *is*. Because one can't escape from that. It's always there, the bundle of passions, weaknesses, stupidities, that one calls character, waiting to trip one up. Look at the governor, that pillar of rectitude and business ability !

[MR. JACKSON *hastily assumes a less commanding posture.*]

206   ACT IV

Do you suppose *he* could be like me if he tried ? Of course not.   Nor could I be like him.

MR. JACKSON.   Have you no will ?

EUSTACE.   No.   Have you ?   Have we any of us ? Aren't we just the creatures of our upbringing, of circumstance, of our physical constitution ?   We are launched on the stream at our birth.   Some of us can swim against the current.   Those who can't it washes away.

[*There is a pause.* HENRY *looks sullen,* MR. JACKSON *puzzled.* EUSTACE, *who has grown rather heated, regains his composure.*]

MR. JACKSON [*with a sigh*].   Well, what's to be done with you ?

EUSTACE [*shrugs*].   I'm afraid you'll have to keep me.   You're my father, you know.   You've brought into the world a worthless and useless human being. I think those were *your* adjectives ?   You're responsible.

MR. JACKSON [*angry again*].   Is that any reason why I should support you ?

EUSTACE [*quite sincerely*].   No, father.   Frankly, I don't think it is.   I think your sensible course would be to put me quietly out of this wicked world or hire some one else to do so.   I'm a bad egg.   I shall never hatch into anything that will do you the smallest credit.   Your sensible course is to destroy me.   But you daren't do that.   Social convention won't allow you.   The law would make a fuss. Indeed, the law won't even allow me to put an end to myself and save you the trouble.   I should be rescued, very wet and draggled, from the muddy waters of the Ched by the solitary policeman who seems to have nothing else to do but to stand about rescuing people who had much better be left to drown. I should be haled before the magistrates— you're a magistrate yourself now, father. You'd be there—I should be given a solemn lecture and then "handed over to my friends"—that's you again, father—who would undertake to look after me in future. And I only hope you would be able to conceal your annoyance at my rescue from the prying eyes of your brother justices !

MR. JACKSON [*stung*]. You've no right to say that. You've no right to suggest that I wish you were dead.

EUSTACE [*genially*]. Of course you do. You want me to go to Australia, where you'll never hear of me again, where, in fact, I shall be dead to you. What's the difference ?

[*A pause.*]

MR. JACKSON. Well, I won't argue with you. The question is, what do you propose ?

EUSTACE [*as if it was the most natural suggestion in the world*]. In the circumstances, I think your wisest course will be to make me an allowance, say three hundred a year, paid quarterly. Then I'll go away and live quietly in London, and you'll be rid of me.

MR. JACKSON [*furious*]. I refuse, sir. I refuse absolutely. The suggestion is utterly shameless.

EUSTACE [*calmly*]. I dare say. But it's perfectly sensible. I appeal to Henry.

HENRY [*after a moment's thought*]. Father, I

think you'd better do as he says. If you gave him a thousand pounds, as we intended, he'd only lose it. Better make him an allowance. Then you can always stop it if he doesn't behave himself. It's a shameless proposal, as you say, but it's practical.

EUSTACE. Bravo, Henry! I always said you had brains. That's it exactly. Shameless, but eminently practical.

MR. JACKSON [*grumbling*]. What I can't see is, *why* I should allow you this money. Here's Henry who's perfectly satisfactory, and has never caused me a moment's anxiety. I don't give *him* money. Whereas you, who have never caused me anything else, expect me to keep you for the remainder of your life.

EUSTACE [*with bitter contempt*]. It is unreasonable, isn't it? But we live in a humanitarian age. We coddle the sick and we keep alive the imbecile. We shall soon come to pensioning the idle and the dissolute. You're only a little in advance of the times. England is covered with hospitals for the incurably diseased and asylums for the incurably mad. If a tenth of the money were spent on putting such people out of the world, and the rest were used in preventing the healthy people from falling sick, and the sane people from starving, we should be a wholesomer nation.

MR. JACKSON [*after a pause*]. Well, if Henry thinks so I suppose I must give you an allowance— but I won't go beyond two hundred.

EUSTACE. I can't keep out of debt on two hundred.

MR. JACKSON. Two hundred and fifty, then.

EUSTACE [*persuasively*]. Three hundred.

MR. JACKSON. Two hundred and fifty. Not a penny more. [*Breaking out again.*] Why, I'd starve before I consented to sponge on my family as you are doing!

EUSTACE [*quietly*]. Ah! You evidently don't know much about starving, father!

[*Silence.* MR. JACKSON *suddenly realises that his son has actually known what hunger means, and the thought makes him uncomfortable.*]

If you write me a cheque for my first quarter now I can catch the 11.15 up.

MR. JACKSON [*almost gently*]. You can't go to-night. . . . You're not packed. . . . And you'll want to say good-bye to your mother.

EUSTACE. I think not. As I'm to go, it had better be as suddenly as I came. It saves such a lot of explanations. You can send my things after me to London.

MR. JACKSON [*sadly*]. Very well. I'll go and write you a cheque.

[MR. JACKSON *goes out with a heavy sigh, and silence falls upon the two brothers. At last* HENRY *speaks.*]

HENRY [*bitterly*]. Well, you've got what you wanted.

EUSTACE [*genially*]. Thanks to you, my dear fellow.

HENRY. And what a sordid plot it has been! To make your way into this house by a trick with the deliberate intention of blackmailing your own father. ·

EUSTACE [*remonstrating good-humouredly*]. You're wrong. The blackmail, as you call it, was an after-thought. When I made my way into this house—in the way you so accurately describe—my designs went no further than getting some decent food and a house over my head for a few days. But when I got here and found you all so infernally prosperous, the governor flinging money about over getting into Parliament, you intending to marry Faring-ford's daughter, I thought I'd better put in for a share of the plunder.

HENRY [*disgusted*]. Well, you've succeeded—succeeded because you've neither honour nor conscience about you.

EUSTACE [*turning on him*]. No. I've succeeded because you're a snob and the governor's a snob, and that put you both in my power. I might have been as poor and as unscrupulous as you please without getting a halfpenny out of either of you. Luckily, the governor's political ambitions and your social ambitions gave me the pull over you, and I used it.

HENRY. Faugh ! [*Turns away angrily, then faces his brother again.*] You understand, of course, that if you are to have this allowance it is on the express condition that you give up all thoughts of Miss Faringford, give them up absolutely.

EUSTACE [*carelessly*]. By all means. What should *I* be about marrying a penniless girl like Stella ?

HENRY. There's nothing you won't do for money ! Even to giving up the girl you pretend to care for.

EUSTACE [*shrugs*]. I dare say. Besides, what

would Stella be about marrying a penniless devil like me ?

HENRY [*exasperated at the injustice of the world*]. And the best of it is, if this story ever gets about, *you'll* get all the sympathy ! Ne'er-do-wells always do. The governor and I would be despised as a couple of stony-hearted wretches with no bowels of compassion, who grudged money to a necessitous brother, while *you* would be called a light-hearted devil-may-care chap who is nobody's enemy but his own.

EUSTACE [*grimly*]. Well, I think I'd change places with you. After all, you're pretty comfortable here. And you'll marry Stella, damn you !

[MR. JACKSON *enters with a cheque in his hand, and* HENRY *is silent.*]

MR. JACKSON [*holding out cheque to* EUSTACE]. Here's your cheque.

EUSTACE [*taking it and reading the amount prosaically*]. Fours into two hundred and fifty. £62 10s. od. Thanks, father. [*Holds out hand.*] Good-bye.

[MR. JACKSON *draws himself up and puts his hands behind his back with awful dignity.*]

You may as well. After all, I'm your son. And if I'm a sweep, it's your fault.

MR. JACKSON [*takes his hand after a moment's hesitation*]. Good-bye.

[EUSTACE *goes slowly towards door.*]

You may write occasionally, just to let us know how you are.

EUSTACE [*offering cheque, with a grim smile*]. Make it three hundred, father—and I won't write.

[MR. JACKSON *is about to protest angrily, then, recognising the uselessness of that proceeding, says nothing, but waves cheque contemptuously away.* EUSTACE, *still smiling, pockets it.*]

No ? Well, have it your own way. Good-bye. Good-bye, Henry. [*Nods to him without offering to shake hands, and goes out as the curtain falls.*]

THE END

PRINTED BY
BALLANTYNE & COMPANY LTD
AT THE BALLANTYNE PRESS
TAVISTOCK STREET COVENT GARDEN
LONDON

ImTheStory.com

Personalized Classic Books in many genre's

Unique gift for kids, partners, friends, colleagues

Customize:

- Character Names
- Upload your own front/back cover images (optional)
- Inscribe a personal message/dedication on the
  inside page (optional)

Customize many titles Including
- Alice in Wonderland
- Romeo and Juliet
- The Wizard of Oz
- A Christmas Carol
- Dracula
- Dr. Jekyll & Mr. Hyde
- And more...